MOTHER ANGELICA'S
GUIDE TO PRACTICAL HOLINESS

Also by Mother Angelica:

Praying with Mother Angelica
Meditations on the Rosary, the Way of the
Cross, and Other Prayers

Mother Angelica's Answers, Not Promises

Mother Angelica on Christ and Our Lady

Mother Angelica on Suffering and Burnout

Mother Angelica's Quick Guide to the Sacraments

Mother Angelica on Prayer and Living for the Kingdom

Mother Angelica on God, His Home, and His Angels

MOTHER ANGELICA'S
GUIDE TO
PRACTICAL
HOLINESS

EWTN PUBLISHING, INC.
Irondale, Alabama

Mother Angelica's Guide to Practical Holiness was originally published as eight mini-books: *Holiness in a Nutshell* (1976), *Holiness Is for Everyone* (1976), *Come, Follow Me* (1976), *Praying into Prayer* (1976), *Two Wills, His and Mine* (1977), *In the Shadow of His Light* (1973), *Holiness in Action* (1976), and *Three Keys to the Kingdom* (1977), copyright Our Lady of the Angels Monastery 3222 County Road 548, Hanceville, Alabama 35077, www.olamshrine.com, and printed with the ecclesiastical approval of Joseph G. Vath, D.D., Bishop of Birmingham, Alabama, USA.

Cover and interior design by Perceptions Design Studio.

Cover art: detail from official portrait by John Howard Sanden.

All quotations from Holy Scripture are taken from Jerusalem Bible, © 1966 by Darton Longman and Todd Ltd. and Doubleday and Company Ltd.

EWTN Publishing, Inc.
5817 Old Leeds Road, Irondale, AL 35210

Distributed by Sophia Institute Press, Box 5284, Manchester, NH 03108.

Library of Congress Cataloging-in-Publication Data

Names: M. Angelica (Mary Angelica), Mother, 1923-2016, author.
Title: Mother Angelica's guide to practical holiness.
Description: Irondale, Alabama : EWTN Publishing, Inc., 2018.
Identifiers: LCCN 2017055236 | ISBN 9781682780107 (hardcover : alk. paper)
Subjects: LCSH: Holiness—Catholic Church. | Christian life—Catholic authors. | Spiritual life—Catholic Church.
Classification: LCC BX2350.3 .M2115 2018 | DDC 248.4/82—dc23 LC record available at https://lccn.loc.gov/2017055236

First printing

Contents

EDITOR'S NOTE

This volume brings together for the first time *Holiness in a Nutshell*; *Holiness Is for Everyone*; *Come, Follow Me*; *Praying into Prayer*; *Two Wills, His and Mine*; *In the Shadow of His Light*; *Holiness in Action*; and *Three Keys to the Kingdom*, eight "mini-books" written by Mother Angelica and published by Our Lady of the Angels Monastery in the 1970s. Each section of this book corresponds to one of Mother's original mini-books. Taken together, they form a unique and beautiful work of spiritual wisdom and prayerful reverence.

Mother Angelica wrote these words on a pad of paper while in Adoration of the Blessed Sacrament in the chapel of her monastery in Irondale, Alabama. Her order, the Poor Clares of Perpetual Adoration, has been dedicated to the Blessed Sacrament since its founding, and so it is only fitting that Mother's written works were completed in His Presence.

By the mid-1970s, the Nuns of Our Lady of the Angels Monastery were printing as many as twenty-five thousand copies of these mini-books and others per day. This was truly a nascent mass-media operation, one that would lead to the creation of EWTN—the Eternal Word Television Network. This book is a faithful representation of Mother Angelica's original work, with only the most basic corrections of printing errors, adjustments to formatting, and so on. You can be confident that you are reading an authentic presentation of the wisdom and spirituality of one of the most important figures in the history of Catholicism in America.

MOTHER ANGELICA'S
GUIDE TO PRACTICAL HOLINESS

Holiness in a Nutshell

To be changed is conversion.
To be transformed is Holiness.

Who Is Called to Be Holy?

All men, women and children of every age, in every state of life, condition, talent and profession.

You are called to holiness.

Be holy in all you do, since it is the Holy One who has called you, and scripture says, "Be holy, for I am holy." (1 Pet. 1:15-16)

Why?

Because God loves you!

You are precious to Him.

You belong to Him.

He loved you before time began. He is your Father.

You need Him.
He wants you to be like Him — holy.

We are God's work of art, created in Christ Jesus to live the good life as from the beginning he had meant us to live it. (Eph. 2:10)

When?
Now! Today — at this moment.
His grace is sufficient for you.

At a favorable time, I have listened to you, on the day of salvation I came to your help. Well, now is the favorable time; this is the day of salvation. (2 Cor. 6:2)

Where Can I Be Holy?
At home
At work
At rest
At school
In a crowd, alone, in your family, in prison, in the ghetto.
Everywhere you can be holy.

Whatever you eat, whatever you drink, whatever you do at all, do it for the glory of God. (1 Cor. 10:31)

Is It Possible?

Yes, Jesus will bear fruit in you if you cooperate with His Grace. Grace comes with repentance, Confession, Communion, prayer, Sacraments, Scripture, Good Works—love, faith and hope.

> We are only earthenware jars that hold this treasure, to make it clear that such an overwhelming power comes from God and not from us. (2 Cor. 4:7)

Is It Really for Me?

Yes, holiness is for you. It is not for specially chosen souls. Holiness is for ordinary people who accomplish God's Will with joy, in faith and in trust.

> The temple of God is sacred; and you are that temple. (1 Cor. 3:17)

What Must I Do?

Be faithful to your state in life—married, single, religious, student.

Be faithful to Holy Mother Church—Precepts, Sacraments, Commandments, Doctrine, Teaching.

Read the Word of God and other spiritual reading.

Follow the Beatitudes—the Blueprint for holiness.
Be loving and concerned.
Let Jesus shine through you. Pray.

Fill your minds with everything that is true, everything that is noble, everything that is good and pure. (Phil. 4:8)

What Are Some Practical Suggestions?

1. See God in the present moment.
2. Turn every disagreeable situation to the good of your soul.
3. Adapt yourself to your neighbor's temperament.
4. Be united to God's Will.
5. Choose God above yourself.
6. Imitate Jesus.
7. Visit Jesus in the Eucharist often.
8. Practice virtue.
9. Frequent the Sacraments.
10. Try to be aware of His Presence.

Each of us should think of our neighbors and help them to become stronger Christians. (Rom. 15:2)

Where Is My Strength?
In the Father's mercy
In the Precious Blood of Jesus
In the power of the Spirit
In the intercession of Mary, our Mother
In the protection of the angels
In the Eucharist
In His Cross.

May Our Lord Jesus Himself and God our Father, who has given us His love, and through His grace, such inexhaustible comfort and such sure hope, comfort you and strengthen you in everything good that you do or say. (2 Thess. 2:16-17)

Will I See Results?
Yes, in more harmony at home
More patience with your neighbor
More strength to overcome weaknesses
More compassion for others
More mercy
More joy
Peace in the midst of turmoil.

What the Spirit brings is love, joy, peace, patience, kindness, goodness, trustfulness, gentleness and self-control. (Gal. 5:22-23)

Where Is My Continuing Source of Holiness?
His Love — His Grace
His Church — His Word
His Spirit — His Power
His Sacraments — His Presence
His Cross — His Resurrection

For My flesh is real food and My blood is real drink. He who eats my flesh and drinks my blood lives in me and I live in him. (John 6:56)

How Long Will It Take?
From moment to moment, from prayer to prayer, from day to day.

Not that I have become perfect yet: I have not yet won, but I am still running, trying to capture the prize for which Christ Jesus captured me. I am far from thinking I have already won. All I can say is that I forget the past and I strain ahead for what is still to come. (Phil. 3:12-16)

Goals
To be like Jesus
To love my neighbor like Jesus does
To be loyal to His Church
To spread the Good News
To be Holy

I have made you a light for the nations, so that my salvation may reach the ends of the earth. (Acts 13:47)

THE CALL TO HOLINESS

Holiness Is for Everyone

The Call

"It is to the glory of my Father that you should bear much fruit, and then you will be my disciples" (John 15:8).

Holiness of life is not the privilege of a chosen few — it is the obligation, the call and the will of God for every Christian.

We cannot put up stumbling blocks of well-defined excuses to reason our way out of the reality that "our sanctification is the Will of God" (1 Thess. 4:3). We were created by God for the express purpose of radiating His Son, Jesus, in our own particular and unique way. We give Him glory by freely choosing to be what His Wisdom designed us to be.

A Christian is to be a "sign of contradiction" (Luke 2:34), a light on top of the mountain, a thorn in the side of the world. His entire life is a silent reproach to sinners, a beacon of hope to the oppressed, a ray of sunshine to the saddened, a source of encouragement to the destitute and a visible sign of the invisible reality of grace.

Saints are ordinary people, who love Jesus, try to be like Him, are faithful to the duties of their state in life, sacrifice themselves for their neighbor and keep their hearts and minds free of this world.

They live in the world, but rise above its mediocre standards. They enjoy living because life is a challenge, not an indulgence. They may not understand the reason for the cross, but faith gives them that special quality to find hope within it. They do understand they are to walk in their Master's footsteps and everything that happens to them is turned to their good.

Saints are ordinary people, who do what they do for the love of Jesus, say what they must say without fear, love their neighbor even when they are cursed by him and live without regret over yesterday or fear of tomorrow.

No one is exempt from the call to holiness. Men, women and children have climbed the ladder of life and reached high degrees of sanctity. These holy Christians have come from every conceivable state and vocation.

There was 9 year old Tarcisus, who defended the Eucharist with his life. Maria Goretti, age 11, defended her virginity as she was stabbed over and over by her assailant. Her sanctity shone brightly when she forgave her murderer and prayed for his conversion.

Mary of Egypt was a prostitute at 16. She joined a group of pilgrims to the Holy Land in an effort to ply her trade. When she reached the Church, an invisible force kept her from entering. Frightened by the experience, she gazed at a statue of Mary and realized the enormity of her sins. She determined to change her life and never again offend God. Forty years later, she died, a woman renowned for her holiness of life.

Matt Talbot was a hopeless alcoholic for most of his life. The disdain of his friends as he stood before them trembling for a drink, awakened his soul to its plight. He changed his life and directed his energies toward being like Jesus and looking toward eternal life.

The saints of the past were human beings with human frailties. St. Jerome had a violent temper and fought against that weakness his entire life. Dismas was a thief, who ended his life with one act of love and repentance and was privileged to have Jesus promise him Paradise. Both Charles de Foucauld and Francis of Assisi were playboys, who finally surrendered to the Hound of Heaven.

Every saint struggled and fought against his weaknesses all his life and as he acquired habits of virtue, he never lost sight of the dying embers of his weaknesses. He conquered by continual vigilance, always aware of what he was and what he could become. This uneasiness as to his own evil capabilities threw him into the arms of God. He depended on Him for everything and gave Him the credit for the least act of virtue in his life.

Men are not born saints with special gifts and privileges. They fight against the world, the flesh and the devil and as they conquer, the Spirit of Jesus begins to shine through with more clarity. We sometimes confuse the particular mission of the saints with their holiness. If compassion were to radiate through one, then healing would be given to that individual to manifest the power of God. But the charism is not part of holiness, it is merely an off-shoot—a gift to be given to others. It was God's gift to the saint for the benefit of the people of God. It is possible to possess charisma and not be holy. We see this clearly in the life of Judas. He spent three years with Jesus and possessed the power to heal, preach and deliver, but he himself did not grow in holiness. His weaknesses were aggravated by the power Jesus gave him for he saw it as a gift that bore his own person and pocketed little profit.

We cannot hide under the cozy excuse of not being chosen — or not possessing special qualities. If we are Christians we have been chosen. If we have been chosen, then those qualities peculiar to the degree of the holiness God calls us to will blossom out as we grow.

A little acorn has no resemblance to the mighty oak it will one day become, but nonetheless, all the material necessary in that giant tree is compressed into a small seed. Time, rain, sunshine, cold and storm are all necessary to bring out the hidden beauty, great height, and strong trunk that will give shade and delight to the heart of man.

Jesus has compared each of us to a seed sown in the soil of His grace. In parable form He described how some of us respond to the Sower's efforts to make us grow. He also described what obstacles prevent us from growing.

Before we see how we can become holy, it may be well to see what reasons Jesus gave for our not arriving at that holy state. We need to dispense with our well-worn excuses and tailor-made objections.

Why We Are Not Holy

"When anyone hears the word of the Kingdom without understanding, the evil one comes and carries off what was sown in his heart. This is the man who received the seed on the edge of the path" (Matt. 13:19). There are many souls on the "edge of the path." They live in the midst of noise and chaos. When any truth begins to take hold of them they merely increase the noise level in their lives and drown out the Word. They truly live on the edge of the path—hearing, but not understanding—filled with the distractions of the world. This type of person sluffs off the idea of sanctity because it means walking in the path of Jesus. He is so comfortable in his own path at the edge, he cannot conceive of a change. The old familiar rut is his home and source of consolation.

"The one who received the word on patches of rock is the man who hears the word and welcomes it at once with joy, but he has no root in him, he does not last; let some trial come, or some persecution on account of the word, and he falls at once" (Matt: 13:20-21). This is the impetuous Christian. He both receives and rejects Christianity "at once." There was a semblance of faith in his mind, but that faith never led to love. When the thrill of being "new-born" wears off, this man easily succumbs in time of trial. He may read the lives of the saints and begin to imagine himself in a state of ecstasy or martyrdom or performing some other heroic deed. In his meditations the big sacrifices come easily, but life is not filled with too many big events in which he can prove his love for God. It is little every day trials that prove love and prune souls. When a man endures the ridicule of his neighbor because of his Christian principles, or intimidation for his orthodox stand in faith and morals, that man suffers persecution. These every day trials prove whether or not the Word has taken "root" in his soul. The question is not whether or not this kind of individual is called to holiness — the question is, what does he do with the events in his life designed to make him holy? Does he endure with faith and grow in love or does he reject, run and resist?

"The one who received the seed in thorns is the man who hears the Word, but the worries of this world and the lure of riches choke the Word and so he produces nothing" (Matt: 13:22). This is certainly a graphic description of the deception filling so many hearts today. What are the worries of this world? Perhaps Jesus was thinking of the man who covets intellectual snobbery, sophisticated attitudes, vanity, and worldly glory—the one who spends his time and energy in the vain pursuit of the things that "moth consumes and rust destroys" (Matt: 6:19). When we add the "lure of riches" to this litany of day dreams, we can easily see why Jesus used the word "choke." These kinds of unrealized desires literally crowd out of the mind and heart the Word of God. It is the call to be humble, poor, chaste, compassionate, guileless, loving and self-sacrificing that is choked out by the consuming fire of self-indulgence, pride, deceit, lust and greed. God spoke the Word meant to give life to one whose ears were opened only to the sound of his own voice.

"And the one who received the seed in rich soil is the man who hears the word and understands it; he is the one who yields a harvest and produces now a hundred-fold, now sixty, now thirty" (Matt: 13:23). This part of the parable explanation that Jesus gave us is encouraging. He is telling us that there will be times we reap much fruit in our lives but there will be other times we do not measure up completely, but we still bear fruit.

Our motives may not be the best, our patience worn thin, our endurance near the end, but Jesus looks for the sign of virtue and goodness so He can bear fruit in us. He takes every scrap of virtue and touches it with His love and it is changed into an eternal reward. His mercy envelops us and reaches into the depths of our souls to renew, change, transform and build.

He brings good out of everything that happens to us as His love builds up everything we do well and reshapes the effects of our failures. His Spirit is always working for our good; nothing is wasted—there are no throwaways, no discards. We are the ones who reject Him—He never rejects us. We think only of perfection, the feeling of a job well done. He looks for deep humility in our hearts, self-knowledge in our minds and effort in our will. He will bear the fruit in us as we grow in our desires and efforts.

The day we realize we have nothing to give Him that is totally ours except our sins and weaknesses—on that day we shall bear a hundred-fold fruit. Only then shall we be empty of our illusions, conscious of our dependence on Him and aware of the reality of His action in our souls. We will take our eyes off ourselves and what we accomplish and keep our eyes on Jesus. We will accept ourselves as we are, striving to be better, conforming our lives to His life, and our will to His Will and our hearts to His Heart.

Those Human Saints

The concept of the perfect, faultless saint is unrealistic. We have only to look at the gospels to see how imperfect the Apostles and first Christians were. There was a point in their lives when they changed. We call that point the time of their "conversion," their encounter with the Sanctifying Spirit. For the Apostles it was Pentecost, for Paul it was a blinding light on the road to Damascus, for Cornelius it was the mere presence of Peter. However, most of the saints did not have dramatic experiences. As we have already seen in the life of Matt Talbot, it was pain, disappointment, and a feeling of emptiness that pushed him into the arms of God. No matter what happened, the saints determined at some point to follow Jesus. A vacuum deep in their souls began to be filled, for they found the pearl of great price. They all changed their lives, some their state in life, but they did not get rid of their weaknesses. They fought harder, conquered more often and grew, like Jesus, "in grace and wisdom before God and men" (Luke 2:52).

In the Acts we see Peter's vacillating spirit making him and everyone else miserable as he took so much time deciding the fate of the Gentiles. Paul's temper flared quickly as he argued his point before the gathering of Apostles. John, called by Jesus a son of thunder, had little patience with those who would not follow Jesus.

In the lives of all the saints we find the following similarities:

- love for God and neighbor,
- determination to imitate Jesus,
- an immediate rising after a fall,
- a complete breakaway from grievous sin,
- growth in virtue and prayer,
- and the accomplishment of God's Will.

These factors are available to every human being; they do not exclude imperfections and faults. We must make a distinction between faults and sins. A saintly person keeps the Commandments; however, he may possess various human qualities, dispositions that make the imitation of Jesus a sanctifying process. These weaknesses make him choose constantly between himself and God. It is in this emptying of oneself and the "putting on of Jesus" that he becomes holy.

Holiness is a "growth experience" and growth consists in advancing in knowledge, love, self-control and all those other imitable virtues of Jesus. We must not lose sight of holiness as we grow, for holiness only means that Jesus is more to us than anyone or anything else in the world. But this desire to belong entirely to God does not exclude being loving to our neighbor, compassionate, caring, patient and kind. Our desire to belong to God enhances all these virtues in our souls, increases our love for our neighbor and makes us more unselfish.

A housewife becomes holy by being a loving wife and mother, filled with compassion for her family because she is filled with the compassionate Jesus.

A husband and father becomes holy by being a good provider, hardworking, honest and understanding because his model is the provident Jesus.

Both husband and wife become holy together as their love for Jesus grows. Love makes them see themselves and change those frailties that are not like their Model. In doing this, life together is less complicated and more loving and understanding. They are bound together by love and prayer, mutual striving and forgiving.

Children become holy by being obedient, thoughtful, joyful and loving. These qualities are maintained by grace and prayer.

Being faithful to the duties of one's state in life and faithful to the grace of the moment are not as easy as they appear. Our temperament, weaknesses, society, work and even the weather clamor for our attention. Living a spiritual life in an unspiritual world and maintaining the principles of Jesus over the principles of this world is hard, but within reach of all. The paradox is that if we choose evil over good it is hell all the way to hell and that is harder.

Christianity is a way of life, a way of thought, a way of action that is contrary to the way of the world. This makes the Christian stand alone and it is this aloneness that discourages him from striving for holiness. However, it is this same aloneness that makes him stand out in a crowd. He becomes a beacon for those who do not enjoy the darkness, a light that enlightens the minds of all around him, a fire that warms cold hearts.

He struggles as all men struggle; he works, eats, sleeps, cries and laughs, but the spirit in which he accomplishes ordinary human needs and demands makes him holy. He does not always make the right decisions but he learns from his mistakes. He does not correspond to every grace, but he accepts his failures with humility and tries harder to be like the Master. He does not condone sin, and though he is ever aware of his own sinner condition, he loves his neighbor enough to correct him with gentleness when his soul is in danger.

He is free to have or have not, for his real treasure is Jesus and the invisible realities. He can possess with detachment or be dispossessed without bitterness.

He knows his Father well enough to entrust his past to His mercy. The Spirit is a friend who guides his steps and straightens the crooked paths ahead. His time and talents are spent in the imitation of Jesus in the ever present now.

The saint is the person who loves Jesus on a personal level; loves Him enough to want to be like Him in everyday life; loves Him enough to take on some of His loveable characteristics. Like Jesus, he lovingly accomplishes the Father's Will, knowing that all things are turned to good because he is loved personally by such a great God.

Let us not be confused by the talents and missions of other Saints. Let us be the kind of saints we were created to be. There are no little or great saints—only men and women who struggled and prayed to be like Jesus—doing the Father's Will from moment to moment wherever they are and whatever they are doing.

Saints are ordinary people with the compassion of the Father in their souls, the humility of Jesus in their minds and the love of the Spirit in their hearts. When these beautiful qualities grow day by day in everyday situations, holiness is born.

The Father gave His Son so we would become His children and heirs of His Kingdom. Jesus was born, lived and died and rose to show us the way to the Father. The Spirit gave us His gifts so we would be clothed with the jewels of virtue, the gold of love, the emeralds of hope and the brilliant diamonds of faith.

Let us not be content with the scotch tape and the aluminum foil of this world.

Be Holy—wherever you are!

Come, Follow Me

You did not choose me, no, I chose you;
and I commissioned you to go out and
to bear fruit. (John 15:16)

Jesus wanted His disciples and all those who would be chosen to follow Him in the future, to understand the essence of their vocation. A vocation to the religious life and in particular to contemplative life, is a special call. It cannot be explained, only accepted. It is a silent voice whose urging creates within the soul a burning desire to know God, to be with God, to serve God and completely dedicate one's total self to God. It is not something the soul decides—it is an acceptance of a choice made by God—it is a courageous gesture of love on the part of the soul and an outpouring of merciful love on the part of God.

Religious life is an encounter with the living God. Sometimes that encounter is preceded by a kind of soul searching agony that tries desperately not to hear, runs in the opposite direction and frantically tries to reason itself out of answering the invitation. This is so because the world has conditioned our minds to believe only what we see and never to venture into the unknown unless success is guaranteed.

In the quotation from St. John, Jesus asked two things — to "go out and to bear fruit" (John 15:16). This going out entails a change of place, work and mission but most of all a change of self. A vocation not only demands a gift of talent, time, possessions, family and friends but a gift of one's own self. "Unless the grain of wheat falls on the ground and dies, it remains only a single grain" (John 12:24). Giving up one's prized possessions and one's self is not as negative as it seems. God does not make demands that leave us in some kind of vacuum. St. Peter asked Jesus what reward would be given those who had left all things for Him and Jesus answered, "Everyone who has left houses, brothers, sisters, father, mother, children or lands for the sake of my name will be repaid a hundred times over and also inherit eternal life" (Matt. 19:29).

A vocation is a gift from beginning to end — a call to rise above the things of this world and prove by a living witness that there is something more and better to come. Those who have been called to this witnessing role are not deprived of love, comfort or joy. They merely find these gifts on a more spiritual and lasting level. Their personalities are not destroyed in some sacrificial act of piety, but developed and made beautiful by the grace of God constantly being poured into their emptying vessels.

Grace builds on nature and, contrary to popular belief, those called by God to be holy in this special way find their identity, fulfill their life, love without limit and are free of attachments. They are not afraid to know themselves, for self-knowledge makes them humble enough and wise enough to realize how very much they need God as Savior and Lord. This realization is the beginning of freedom—the door to holiness—the entrance to the Temple of God.

To assure themselves of this self-knowledge and positive growth in holiness, those called by God to be religious bind themselves to live in community and consecrate their most prized possessions—the faculties of their souls—by the three vows of Poverty, Chastity and Obedience. The Vows are not Chains that bind, but Keys that open—they are not things sacrificed, but gifts received—they are not privations that warp, but freedoms that deliver—they are not the myrrh of penance, but the incense of sacrifices lovingly ascending to the throne of God. The purified faculties are like three rings, each more beautiful than the other, ever growing in value and brilliance as they reflect more and more the Source from which they come — God.

These thoughts are not poetic ramblings about some impossible ideal, but the obligation of everyone to whom God has given a religious vocation. A religious is to be a "Light in the Darkness" (John 1:5) — a "city on top of the mountain" (Matt. 5:14) for all men to see and praise their God. It is for His Glory they are to "shine like stars," not their own. A religious is a special envoy from God to the world and irrespective of the mission entrusted to them, their union with God is their greatest work. Religious are more than workers in the Lord's vineyard — they are friends who are tied to the Master of the vineyard by the bonds of friendship — friendship that is powerful in its intercessory role. This role is more important than any amount of work accomplished and we find this explained by Jesus when He said, "If you remain in me and my words remain in you, you may ask what you will and you shall get it. It is to the glory of my Father that you should bear much fruit and then you will be my disciples" (John 15:7-8). We who are religious, or those who will be called to that state, must keep in mind the importance of bearing fruit before we distribute that fruit to our neighbor. We cannot give what we do not possess. It is not enough to be servants who distribute the Master's goods. We are to be disciples, who bring in the sick, lame, crippled, blind and deaf and seat them at the Master's table — not for some temporary handout, but an ongoing banquet of good things for them to permanently feed their souls upon. St. Paul tells us the Word of God is "living and active — like a two-edged sword" (Heb. 4:12). The fruit a religious is to bear is the glimpse of Jesus he or she gives to the world by their imitation of Jesus. Whatever mission flows from that wellspring of holiness is secondary. Whether that mission is teaching, nursing, social work or intercessory contemplative prayer, it cannot be substituted for the witnessing role of a life of holiness. The Father is glorified when a poor, weak creature, made in His image, yields itself so completely to the sanctifying power of the Spirit, that a "reflection turns to transformation" (2 Cor. 3:18). When the poor are fed the food so necessary for the body, they cannot be deprived of the food so crucial for the soul — the example of a religious who is a breathing image of the love, mercy and compassion of Jesus. To give them one without the other is only to make them poorer and deprive them of God-given rights when they already suffer the privation of human rights. We have been promised by Jesus that we would always have in our midst disciples whose lives would prove His love and Lordship. "With me in them," He said, "and you in me, may they be so completely one that the world will realize that it was you who sent me and that I have loved them as much as you loved me" (John 17:23). The personal and communal life of every religious must exemplify this union with the Trinity—a union that encircles the world with love—the same love with which they are encircled. Without this union with God, the religious only fulfills part of his vocation, and may one day see the reality behind St. Paul's awesome statement. "If I give away all I possess, piece by piece, and if I even let them take my body to burn it, but am without love, it will do me no good whatever" (1 Cor. 13:3).

Religious are not better than other men—they are chosen for the benefit of mankind and the glorification of God on earth. Men climb mountains, scale heights, venture into the unexplored to prove to other men it can be done. This is the witness of today's disciples—they provide a needed witness that holiness is possible in today's world because there is one whose Indwelling Presence accomplishes the difficult, the impossible and the miraculous — a change of life, ideals and goals. Let us look briefly and see how the Spirit works in the soul that has been chosen for this way of life.

The Vow of Poverty

> *None of you can be my disciple unless he gives*
> *up all his possessions. (Luke 14:33)*

The Vow of Poverty purifies the faculty of the intellect, promoting a growth in Faith and producing the fruit of detachment, patience, humility and long-suffering.

Though there are few religious who suffer from want, their Vow of Poverty obliges them to give all they possess to the religious family they join. It is a total dependence on a community for every need in life and a deterrent against greed, superfluities, avarice and worldliness. In the world a poor man may be rich in desires, but the Vow of Poverty strips one of those legitimate desires to possess — those human rights to own property, dispose of possessions and make decisions regarding lifestyle. The renunciation of these interior rights to possess, frees the soul from complicated ambitions and goals that weigh the soul down like a ball and chain. The intellect is free to ponder the mysteries of God for it is no longer entangled in the reasoning, cunning and shrewd intellectual battles that occupy the mind as it seeks to keep what it possesses and acquire more. This necessitates a constant growth in Faith, for when "things" are taken away from the soul, then one sees oneself in a mirror, wiped clean of the dust of possessions, dependent upon superiors and fellow religious, and the privations incumbent to communal living promote a growth in humility and patience. Mutual forbearance of human weaknesses is a major part of the Vow of Poverty for it makes one forget oneself for the good of others. The constant demand to change is to empty oneself like Jesus did. The Vow of Poverty is a daily death, but also a daily resurrection, for every part of us given is replaced by more of Jesus. This is like breathing the air of eternity—free, pure and unimpeded by any particles of possessions.

This Vow reaches down into the depths of the soul and requires a generous gift of one's time, talents, strength, love, virtue and even life if necessary. The soul truly living the Vow of Poverty lives and gives completely as the Spirit leads in the present moment. Yes, this Vow goes beyond things and reaches the depths of one's being—permitting one to sacrifice for God and neighbor. Then it is that the soul reaps the fruit of the first Beatitude, "Blessed are the poor in spirit for theirs is the Kingdom of Heaven." Freedom of spirit makes the soul cry out, "I have been crucified with Christ and I live not with my own life but with the life of Christ who lives in me. The life I now live in this body I live in Faith—faith in the Son of God who loved me and sacrificed himself for my sake" (Gal. 2:19-21).

The Vow of Chastity

> *It is not everyone who can accept what I have said,*
> *but only those to whom it is granted. . . .There*
> *are eunuchs who made themselves that way for*
> *the sake of the kingdom of heaven. Let anyone*
> *accept this who can. (Matt. 19:11-12)*

The Vow of Chastity purifies the Memory, promoting growth in Hope and bearing the fruit of joy, trust, childlikeness, mercy and compassion.

A eunuch in Our Lord's day was completely dedicated to the service of the Queen. He was chosen to live a celibate life so his attention would not be divided. There was, in these pagan times, a deep realization that the affairs of state could brook no competition. The very heart of the eunuch had to belong to the Queen in order for his mind to be undivided by desires and goals other than hers. No one questioned the sovereignty of the Queen who made such demands, and yet there are many who question the right of God to make such requests. Unlike the royalty of old, God, who gave us free will, requests, calls and gives grace when His mission on earth demands one's total attention by a celibate life. This is why Jesus ended His teaching about continence by saying, "Let anyone accept this who can" (Matt. 19:12).

The Vow of Chastity, like Poverty, goes much deeper than the privation of a spouse and children. It is a call from God to arrive at such a degree of holiness that a never ending flood of love issues from the heart to the world. A love like to God's love — unhampered by the necessity of worrying about oneself, about tomorrow or providing for the future. God has a right to call some of His creatures, elevate them by grace and then put them in various positions in life in which they can radiate His unselfish love to the world. He does neither the one He calls nor the world any injustice. He knows the faith of many is enhanced only by seeing visible fruit of His existence in a fellow human being. He also knows that His children need examples of self-control, dedication, zeal and selflessness if they are going to lead virtuous lives. The Vow of Chastity leaves the soul unencumbered by the flesh in the same way the Vow of Poverty releases the soul from the world.

The religious who observes the Vow of Chastity is free to love every human being with the love of Jesus. It purifies the faculty of Memory, for the pleasures, enticements and inordinate desires are held in control. Legitimate human rights to possess a family of one's own are offered to God as a sacrifice of praise. This sacrifice covers the world and then it is that the words of Jesus become a reality. "There is no one who has left house, brothers, sisters, father, children or land for my sake ... who will not be repaid a hundred times over, houses, brothers, sisters, mothers, children and lands—not without persecutions—now in this present life" (Mark 10:29-30). One does not give up love through the Vow of Chastity but one does give up exclusive loves for the gift of possessing an all embracing love. The heart of the celibate is strong enough to be on fire with zeal for God and Kingdom, large enough to embrace all mankind, warm enough to give without receiving in return, trusting enough to forgive without limit, peaceful because God's Will is its only goal, persevering because it is not its own end, courageous because it grows more beautiful in sacrifice and serene because it always possesses its Beloved. The Vow of Chastity truly frees the heart to love, because its Beloved is ever faithful. The religious has no fear of loss, for its Treasure is within—no sense of insecurity for its Beloved is all provident, no jealousy for it is the object of His total love. Yes, the religious who is faithful to the Vow of Chastity has a heart full of love—"pressed down, shaken together, running over" (Luke 6:38) for its Source of love is infinite and has free reign in that soul.

The Vow of Obedience

> My food is to do the will of the one who sent
> me, and to complete his work. (John 6:34)

The Vow of Obedience purifies the faculty of the Will, promoting a growth in Love and bearing the fruit of self-control, courage, meekness, peace, serenity and perseverance.

The most freeing of all the Vows is the Vow of Obedience. This is not because someone else makes decisions and the religious merely follows directions. The role of the superior is not one of dictatorship and Jesus made this very clear. "Among pagans," He said, "it is the kings who lord it over them... this must not happen to you. No; the greatest among you must behave as if he were the youngest, the leader as if he were the one who serves" (Luke 22:25-26). Obviously if a leader is to be a servant the directions he gives are not to be difficult or authoritative. The religious subject has a right to receive humble commands if humble obedience is to be given. However, obedience to lawful authority is only part of the Vow of Obedience — it is in reality the effect or fruit of its more positive aspect, an aspect without which the Vow can become merely an escape from personal responsibility or a charade of external piety.

The religious with this Vow witnesses to the world of the reality of the Presence of God in the present moment. It is the Vow of union and sanctity for it looks for every opportunity to unite the Will of the religious with the Will of God as it makes itself known in the present moment. Like Jesus, the Will of the Father is its daily food — a food unknown to the earthly and worldly. Obedience strengthens the Will because it is constantly being freely exercised and made strong by its adherence to the Will of God in the present moment. The soul of the religious, faithful to the Vow, strives to see God in everything and in everyone. The Will is ever seeking the many daily opportunities to be like Jesus, to overcome its weaknesses, to become strong and free — free of rebellion — free of doubt, free of anger, free of the tensions of that inner struggle seeking to do one's own will.

Not only does Obedience free the soul in regard to itself, but also in regard to one's neighbor. We often rebel at the actions, sufferings, pain, injustice and trials in the lives of others. To do what one can to alleviate the pain of others and then be at peace with the Will of God in their regard is also part of this Vow. A religious bears witness to the world that accomplishing God's Will, manifested in lawful authority, in one's duties, state in life and in the present moment, is possible, sanctifying, freeing, holy and fruitful.

It is Love — love of God and neighbor, that is the power behind such a Will. As love increases through courageous perseverance, serenity and peace fill the soul to overflowing. Truly, the obedient are blest for they see the Father in the present moment and imitate Jesus in every action as their hearts are ever open to the Spirit of Love.

In order to be faithful to these high ideals, the religious must daily grow in a greater participation in the Divine Nature — in grace. The Vows empty the soul in order for God to fill it with Himself. There should be a constant "emptying-filling" process of growth until the soul and God are one.

Just as there are three Vows to empty the soul, there are three sources of grace to fill it. The Vow of Poverty empties the soul of possessions as Scripture fills the soul with the Word of God—its sole possession. The Vow of Chastity empties the soul of an exclusive love as it is filled with the all embracing love in the Eucharist. The Vow of Obedience empties the soul of self-will as it is filled with the courage obtained by Unceasing Prayer.

Yes, the Vows of Poverty, Chastity and Obedience nourished by Scripture, the Eucharist and Prayer, increase Faith, Hope and Love, purify the Memory, Intellect and Will as union with the Father, Son and Holy Spirit grows brighter and brighter for all the world to see.

GROWING IN HOLINESS

PRAYING INTO PRAYER

Love has been defined, analyzed, explained and excused. It has been the cause of wars, feuds, heroism, martyrdom, inordinate passion and beautiful friendships. It pulls two people of opposite temperaments together into a married state and permits them to live happily. It makes friends understand each other without the necessity of words.

Love is an emotional feeling on a human level and a faith experience on a supernatural level. It motivates our wills and enables us to attempt the impossible for the good of His kingdom.

Love fills and empties simultaneously. It makes us reach out to God, ready to be pruned, recklessly desiring whatever the cost. It soothes the aching heart and then makes it thirst for more.

When the longing for God is seemingly satisfied by some joy, that very joy increases the longing and a bitter-sweetness enters our souls. We desire His Presence to fill the void but find the void ever deeper when His Presence is not felt. Those who endeavor to live a spiritual life—an interior life—a life with God in their souls, truly desire but one thing and that is to be united to the object of their love—God. The struggles of daily living seem geared to choking that interior life and snatching it out of our reach.

The harder we try to live a life of loving union, the more difficulties we encounter. We find the various temperaments of those with whom we live and work an obstacle—we find God so far away—we find our determination to be holy short-lived and vacillating. To add to our distress, we read passage after passage from Scripture that demands the highest union—impossible attitudes of mind and heart. Our faith tells us God cannot command the impossible and yet how can we ever begin to follow the new commandment? "This is my commandment," Jesus said, "love one another *as* I love you." ... "As the Father has loved me, so I love you" (John 15:12).

We are asked by Jesus to love our neighbor as much as the Father loves the Son! What an awesome commission—what trust Jesus has in us!

The word "as" means equal to or in the same way and yet we find such a difference between our love and God's love.

Creature love is finite, selfish, limited, vacillating.

God's Love is Infinite, Selfless, Limitless, Constant.

Many of us use God's love like the manna in the desert. We take what we need for particular situations and then go our own way—thinking we can handle other situations ourselves. The soul looks at God as holiness, then at itself and sees sins, frailties and weaknesses. It looks at its neighbor and sees, for the most part, opportunities for the practice of virtue. We reach up to God asking for help and the realization of His holiness mirrors our own unworthiness. The self-knowledge that comes from our daily encounter with our neighbor makes us rebel or feel inferior. We run in an unending triangle from petitioning God for help, to receiving strength to endure, to adapting ourselves to the demands of our neighbor.

We fear God and punishment and expect reward for any good we accomplish. On this level it is difficult to see the Gospel message as Jesus gave it to us. Though we ourselves are sinners, we expect perfection from our neighbor and mercy from God for ourselves.

There is a continual struggle on the part of the soul to keep any kind of serenity or peace. Love, as we find it in God, seems out of our reach and the ability to love our neighbor as

God loves him seems an impossible task. We practice virtue in varying degrees depending on how strong the adverse feeling within us happens to be.

There is great advantage to this stage of the spiritual life. Though we seem to be on a treadmill—going nowhere fast—we are acquiring both natural and supernatural self-knowledge. Natural self-knowledge comes with the awareness of our weakness. For example, when we *feel* impatience—it becomes a part of our physical being. We react as we feel—we know we have offended our neighbor but we often blame our neighbor for bringing out our weaknesses. The emphasis at this stage is more on our neighbor's weaknesses causing us to react in a faulty way. Neighbor becomes "cause" and we suffer from the effects of that cause. Our prayers are turned toward God in supplication to change our neighbor and give us the strength to endure. Self-knowledge at this level tends to place most of the blame for our own actions on others. This can be very frustrating because our time is spent in waiting for others to improve and expecting some special grace that will enable us to be totally indifferent to everything around us. Though we are running around in a vicious circle we begin to realize the uselessness of spending so much time on circumstances and dispositions beyond our control.

When we realize we cannot change our neighbor except through love and example, we seek new ways of prayer—new secrets of the spiritual life that will enable us to overcome. This is the work of supernatural self-knowledge. When, in the midst of some failure to respond to demands of the present moment, we receive a light that makes us see ourselves, see God's pruning hand, see future good in present turmoil, then we are experiencing supernatural self-knowledge. The emphasis shifts from neighbor to self. This is not done so as to make us feel guilty or inferior. This self-knowledge is from God's Spirit. It brings acknowledgment of our weakness, repentance, compassion for self and neighbor, determination to do better and a deeper love for God whose grace gives us light to see truth without flinching. There is no resentment towards our neighbor. We realize that no matter what the cause, our temperament and weaknesses are the real cause of our reaction to adversity. Our neighbor may cause a demand on our virtue, but we ourselves are the cause of our response to that demand. We see this clearly in a situation where three or more people are involved. The response of each will be totally different. One may become angry, another be indifferent and still another be in the dark as to anything happening at all.

Supernatural self-knowledge enables the soul to be attuned to the needs of others and at the same time aware of what response is best suited to the occasion. It looks at the soul almost as a third person, honestly evaluating its weaknesses, loving with the love of Jesus and dying to itself in order to witness to Jesus' love for another.

There is no time wasted hiding from oneself or being guilty over the constant effort needed to be good. Natural self-knowledge has a tendency to engage in self-pity and discouragement but the honest acceptance of one's weaknesses comes from the Spirit and bears the fruit of the Spirit. The Spirit uses our weaknesses and the effort we put forth to increase our *longing* for God, *empty* our souls of inordinate self-love and create a *loneliness* that can only be satisfied by God. These three effects of longing, emptiness and loneliness develop a *thirst* for God in the soul. The fourth beatitude takes up residence in the soul. "Blessed are those who hunger and thirst for what is right: they shall be satisfied" (Matt. 5:6).

Thirst for God is a desire to possess Him with all our heart. The pain of thirsting for God is purifying and meritorious. It increases the soul's capacity for God—for love—for grace. The soul is at this point seeking ways and means of acquiring more knowledge of God. It reads Scripture, performs acts of kindness, frequents the Sacraments, prays more fervently and seeks opportunities to be virtuous. Devotion to the Eucharist and Mary increase as the soul's desire for God becomes almost unbearable.

Humility of heart is a continuous source of strength and the soul begins to increase in trust. In the past the soul's prayer life was more of a struggle — a struggle with past sins and mistakes, present trials and sufferings and future events. Petition and reparation were almost the only goal of the soul's prayer to God. Without realizing it the soul is slowly changed by the Spirit and directed to new ways of prayer and union. Trust, rooted in Hope, enables the soul to give its past and present *to* God and place its future *in* God. Trusting *to* God is to place everything and everyone in His Mercy and Providence with complete confidence. Trusting *in* God is to have the assurance that our loving Father will take care of us and our loved ones.

Trust and Hope release the soul from fear and disperse the clouds that so often make Faith difficult. Faith that is only an intellectual assent to truth can make a soul complacent, satisfied that all is well and there is no need to grow in something one already possesses. Is this perhaps the reason so many who profess their Faith do not advance in the interior life?

Living Faith gives the soul the ability to see God in everything. It raises us above the sense feeling level and permits us to touch God in our daily lives. The trials that increase Hope make us humble and thereby purify Faith in the soul. St. Paul assures us that Faith "proves the existence of the realities that at present remain unseen" (Heb. 11:1). The ability to extract from the present moment the Presence of a loving Father, is a living Faith. When our souls become more and more aware of that Presence we grow in Faith. When Faith becomes so strong that no adversity can quench its growth in the soul, then that soul is well advanced in loving as God loves.

Faith detaches the soul from the necessity of having constant proofs of God's providence and care; of positive answers to all our prayers; and of a need for consolations. It assures us of His pleasure in us and destroys the fear of dryness and desolation. The soul of faith believes because of God's word and that word bears the fruit of love.

When Hope sees good and Faith sees God in the present moment, in oneself and in one's neighbor, Love is pure and selfless. It is an exchange of love between the soul and God with neighbor as the recipient of the overflow. The exchange of love between Father and Son in the Trinity is the Holy Spirit. The Spirit is a power—the Spirit is Love. At Baptism we begin to participate in the Nature of God. In a mysterious fashion the Trinity makes Its home in us. The Father implants Hope in our memory and lives there, the Son implants Faith in the Intellect and lives there and finally the Spirit implants Love in the Will and lives there.

It is important to understand that as we feed the Memory through grace with compassion and mercy towards self and neighbor, the image of the soul resembles Jesus in a more perfect way. Humility and meekness free the soul from an inordinate attachment to its own opinions and will, leaving the soul open to seeing the Father in everything. It gives the Intellect the ability to discern the Father's will and paves the way for the soul to make right choices.

As Jesus kept His eyes ever on the Father, our soul should ever seek what the Father desires of it. The Scriptures, the Church, the Commandments and the precepts all enlighten the Intellect to motivate the Will to live in the Spirit—to live in Love. Jesus consistently asked us to do the Father's Will, to love the Father, to love our neighbor as much as the

Father loves Him, to make our home in Him *as* He makes His home in us.

We should make an effort to be aware of the marvelous work being accomplished in our souls. God the Father is loving God the Son and that mutual Love, which is the Spirit, lives in each soul in grace as in a temple. The Trinity truly lives and loves in the grace-filled soul.

If we were more aware of what is happening within us — if we could close the eyes of our senses long enough to take joy in God loving God in us, we would perhaps begin to absorb that love and share it with our neighbor.

If any soul would develop a habit of being aware of the Father within it, loving Jesus in every human being the soul meets, would not that soul make giant strides in holiness? Would it not look upon everyone with new eyes and new love? Would it not treat everyone as Jesus? Would it not understand in a new way that whatever it does to its neighbor it does to Jesus? It would truly begin to love as God loves. Its inner life and exterior life would be Jesus-centered, God-fearing and full of love.

The soul that follows closely the Trinitarian life within it and patterns its own life accordingly, will love as God loves.

"Father may they be one in us as you are in me and I am in you" (John 17:21).

The three faculties of the soul in grace—Memory, Intellect and Will—enjoy the Divine Indwelling. As it becomes more one with each Person of the Trinity, the soul is slowly transformed. A soul living in God as God lives in it, draws all mankind into its heart. It loves with God's own love because the soul and God have become one. "You will understand," Jesus said, "that I am in the Father and you in me and I in you" (John 14:20).

Let us often contemplate the wonder of the Father loving His Son in us. Let our hearts, overflowing with love, give the Father the joy of loving His Son in our neighbor through our eyes, our touch, our concern, our compassion and our hearts.

TWO WILLS, HIS AND MINE

Attitudes

The most awesome gift God has given each human being is freedom of Will—the ability to accomplish—to act—to say yes or no to temptation, to the call of holiness, to any state in life and even to God.

Hell is a place of the eternal "No" to God by those whose Wills are forever set against Him. The Will is truly an awesome gift when it can reject its Creator.

There are some who boast of having a "strong" will and others who pretend they possess a weak one.

People who have acquired a habit of sin say they cannot stop when in reality they *will* not stop.

A strong Will can drive a man to extremes in any field and give him the strength and courage to do the impossible.

Will power is man's greatest gift and both God and Satan strive to possess it. God says "Unite it to Mine and I will give you Heaven" and Satan says, "Give it to me and I will give you the world." The one is an eternal life of joy, the other an eternity of misery and both are acquired by an act of the Will.

God strives to strengthen man's Will by suffering, trials and disappointments. The crosses in our lives provide the necessary tools that shape and reshape our Wills. The opposite is true of the Enemy. Satan strives to give us everything we desire whenever we desire it. His approach is to say, "do as you please when you please," knowing that our Will is weakened each time we oppose the Author of all Good.

God asks us to unite our Will to His. Since He is Goodness and Wisdom Itself, by conforming our moment to moment existence to His plan, we become holy, happy and develop a strong Will — one that is united to God. It is a matter of two Wills becoming one Will. If a spark becomes one with a fire, it disappears completely and all one sees is a brilliant blaze. What was in itself a mere flicker becomes a light for all to see.

Jesus was constantly reminding His Apostles that the path to holiness was a matter of a union of Wills — God's and the soul's. Of Himself He said, "I have come from heaven not to do my own Will, but the Will of the One who sent Me" (John 6:38).

This then is the role of every human being. The Father gave us all a power to say yes or no to Him. In a deliberate choice between ourselves and Him, we have the power to make ourselves one with Him by accepting His Will or to stand alone by doing our own Will.

A spark that is flung away from the fire soon dies out, for its source of heat and energy is gone. When we unite our Will to the Will of God, we share in His love and that love in us bears fruit in abundance. This act of self-sacrifice makes us a part of everything that is good. On the other hand, when we reject the Will of God, we stand alone, subject to the temptation of the Enemy and drinking deeply of the bitter water of our own selfishness. We become like a man alone in a rudderless boat, desperately trying to steer a straight course with his hands on a single oar.

Man's entire life—his moment to moment existence—is made up of choices. His thoughts and actions are constantly being directed by a powerful Will. No matter what thought crosses his mind, it is his Will that decides whether or not it resides there or whether it will be rejected. No matter how difficult or tedious a task may be, it is the Will putting forth effort that brings success.

There is no weakness of character that cannot be overcome if the person in question *wills* to change. There is no tendency to sin that cannot be controlled if the Will is strong.

Men often fail to become holy, not because they lack talent, but because they lack the Will Power to persevere. We do not become holy because we do not *want* to be holy.

A people can become enslaved under the powerful will of a dictator because they have no will to resist. A dictator can possess the Will of an entire nation to the point of deciding life and death.

A strong Will is something admirable, but if that Will is uncontrolled, it becomes a vehicle for evil. A lack of mental discipline relaxes Will Power and causes us to live entirely on an emotional level. Feelings become the deciding factor in our lives instead of Reason. We become slaves of our own emotions. The earthly trinity of me, myself and I becomes the ruling force of every circumstance. Selfishness and self-indulgence are the desire of the present moment.

This type of existence builds an impenetrable wall around us and no matter where we turn we see only ourselves. Everything is measured by that image. Without a thought of anything but self, the entire world becomes only as large as the fortress we have built around ourselves. We see injustice everywhere because no one possesses the same image of ourselves that we do. The fire of anger ever burns brightly because others who live on a Reason level do not agree with us.

An unbridled Will can lead to a life of frustration and strife. A spirit of arrogance and rebellion are the fruits of an uncontrolled Will.

It is indeed a strange power that can lead a man to extremes—to the heights of sanctity, to the depths of hell, to fame and to misfortune.

Every human being has at some time or other clashed with the Will of God or the Will of other men. We seldom think as others do or share the same opinions. The result of this constant clash of ideas can result in a stronger adherence to our own Will. We can nourish our Will much as a woman nourishes her baby. A constant diet of self-will feeds our pride and the result is the same as overeating—our pride grows out of proportion to our intelligence and the result is disastrous. We make unreasonable demands and become slaves to ourselves.

We can create our own concentration camp where we are both jailer and prisoner, prosecutor and defendant, oppressor and oppressed. Our will can make life a heaven or hell and only we have the power to choose one or the other path.

Men may make demands, nations require sacrifices and society place restrictions on us, but in the final analysis we decide whether we meet demands, make sacrifices or are constrained by restrictions.

No man is perfectly free. He must abide by civil laws that keep order in a disordered society. Refusal to obey those laws causes penalties in one way or another. Everywhere we go there is someone telling us what to do and promising some disastrous result if we do not comply. We are told by labels how to wash clothing, press suits, bake cakes, fix washers and set clocks.

We are advised how to use an electric blanket, take medicine, eat meals, lie in the sun and survive in the desert. We are forced to listen to loud music in public places, jack hammers, jet planes and police sirens.

Newsmen and publishers decide what we hear and what we read. Unknown to us our Wills are constantly being influenced, directed and sometimes forced into action.

We accept all this with a kind of numb serenity. We are half aware of this outside influence, half unconcerned and totally willing to accept the inevitable.

We are willing to be imposed upon by everyone but God. When He demands anything against our Will, we rebel at the injustice of this infringement on our freedom.

We never question the right of civil authority to impose punishment for crimes committed — especially when we are the victims. However, we question the right of God to correct our erring ways and rebel at the pain incurred.

Men lose fortunes in business, gambling and other enterprises and begin again with hope and confidence, but if God takes away a loved one to enjoy a better life, or health to increase eternal glory, they balk, despair and lose heart.

What do we call an attitude where man is right and God is wrong — where man knows what is best for him and God does not — where man is the ruler of his own destiny and God merely an onlooker? We call that attitude Pride and when man's Will is proud — it will not follow — it leads itself into whatever path it pleases. Self-Will becomes the ruling factor of life and God's Will is rejected. Self-Will is a dim guiding light and is bright only to those who live in darkness.

This tendency to live by our own light is in the heart of every human being. We prefer to see something real, to accomplish something visible and to determine a course of action with foreseeable results. To patiently wait for an Invisible God to plan and execute our present and future, is difficult for our human nature. Without grace from God, it would be impossible to attain that Faith so necessary to release our lives and future to His Provident care — to believe that what is happening to us at this moment is in our best interests.

Though our feelings may rebel and our Intellect be unable to comprehend God's Will, it is only important that we accomplish that Will.

We should work towards the day when we will actually desire and want only God's Will in our lives, but we must be patient with ourselves as we fall and stumble toward holiness, as we vacillate in motive and purpose, and as we strive and yet consistently fall away from our best resolutions.

The Struggle

Man is capable of heroic sacrifice and he accomplishes these feats of endurance best when he wants to do them with all his heart. Sacrifices that are imposed against his Will rob him of the spirit so necessary to do great things. A mother thinks nothing of caring for a sick child day and night. A stranger would feel it a great sacrifice. He would not manifest those tender acts of thoughtfulness that make nursing so Christlike.

Love moves the Will in whatever direction love takes. If our love is self-oriented, our actions will be geared toward self-satisfaction only. Unless our Will is directed toward a higher good, we shall not reach our potential. No matter what great things we accomplish in the world it will be as nothing if our motive for good and great works is selfish.

St. Paul reminded us of this when he said that if we gave everything we possessed to the poor without love it would be nothing. It is disheartening to realize it is possible to deprive ourselves of our most prized possessions and it is as nothing before God. Certainly our Will is determined and strong when we accomplish good works. How then could it be nothing in the Eyes of God? (1 Cor. 13:3).

The struggle within does not lie in the strength of our Will but in the prime mover of that Will. What is our motive for doing what we do?

Jesus told us that if we do good works to be seen by men we have received our reward (Matt. 6:1-2). What were Jesus and Paul telling us when they pulled the rug from under our complacent attitudes?

They were both saying the same thing and we need to see why it is possible to be kind and generous and not be doing the Will of God. Certainly kindness and generosity are fruits of the Spirit, but they can also be natural fruits—fruits of our own desire for praise and glory.

The guiding force of all our actions should be to please God, manifest our love for Him and aid our neighbor.

Whatever self-gratification there may be in our works it is secondary—a fringe benefit enjoyed but not sought after. The determining factor is the love of God, not personal glory. This is difficult to attain and only His grace can make us rise above ourselves and seek only Him.

When our Will is directed to the honor and glory of God above our own, we have peace of mind. The constant friction between our Will and God's leads to most of the unhappiness in our lives. We can understand this better if we draw a verbal picture of ourselves alienated from His Will.

Following Our Own Will

In the parable of the Prodigal son we find an excellent example of Self-Will. Here we see a son who demands his inheritance before the father's death. The boy had deliberated a long time and insisted that he be given his share immediately. His Will was set on fun and games and he refused to work and labor long years before he could enjoy his father's wealth. This seemed logical and reasonable to him and this false sense of righteousness made him more and more determined to get his due and leave home.

He began to experience a strange sense of freedom—an arrogant freedom built on possessions, an uncontrolled freedom that was like a runaway horse. He accumulated friends quickly and then, tiring of them, found others who pleased him more.

Every twinge of conscience was smothered by more "riotous" living. He justified every action by inventing new phrases that made everything he did seem right. Drinking was "real living," dissipation became "his human nature," lying and cheating became a "battle of wits," lording over the weak became "survival of the fittest," goodness became "obnoxious and old-fashioned," arrogance became "strength" and irresponsibility became the "freedom to do as he pleased."

This state of body and soul was soon a way of life and all went well for a short time. There were times, no doubt, when his better nature reproached him and a weak call to change took hold of his heart, but any desire to be better was quickly subdued and he went on day after day in "riotous living" (Luke 15:13). Finally, when his money was gone, his popularity diminished. He was in need — he could no longer fulfill the selfish cravings of his friends. One by one they left him and any plea for help on his part was met with scorn and rejection. Only then did he look into his will and see the direction he had taken — only then did he see the folly of his ways — only then did his soul long for the warmth of his father's love — the security of home and the abundant table of his father's house.

His reason returned and he realized that his father's servants were better off than he in every way. Suffering began to do the work that affluence had destroyed. His Will began to guide his life with a properly directed Reason. His poverty cleared the fog of his emotions and he could see the world and himself in a new light.

This account is not far-fetched today for there are many in this state of dissipated living — enslaved "freedom," uncontrolled passions, and lethargic indifference — and only the suffering of privation and failure will set their feet on the right path and direct their Will to their Father.

The battle of Wills rages on between man and God, goodness and evil, love and hate. The question is—who tells us what to do? Whose voice do we listen to? Who directs our steps? Whose example is a guiding power in our lives? We desire to be the master of our fate and sole director of our lives as we are totally unaware of our inabilities, the enemies that surround us or the path to follow.

The Influence

Outside forces beyond our control continually battle for our Will and attention. Our Human Nature seeks its own satisfaction in everything. The *World* besieges us with false attitudes and the *Enemy* seeks ever to deceive us by giving evil the appearance of good. It may be well to look at these three influences to see how they affect our lives.

THE WORLD

"I passed my word on to them and the world hated them because they belong to the world no more than I belong to the world. I am not asking you to remove them from the world but to protect them from the evil one" (John 17:14-15).

We must make a distinction between the "world," meaning our immediate surroundings and the attitudes of mankind in the world.

As God created His "world," Genesis tells us that after each "day," each epoch, God saw that it was good — it still is good. The seasons as they come and go, timed by an invisible clock, thrill our souls. Mountains and waterfalls make us stand in awe at the grandeur of God. The sun and moon are like silent sentinels guarding us from darkness and cold. All this good and the thought of leaving it at death makes both saint and sinner feel lonely, but these things do not constitute the "world" for they are all inanimate creatures.

It is the attitudes of people that constitute the "world" and it is this collective attitude of a particular part of the world that decides the ungodly spirit that permeates the conscience of men and turns them away from God. This collective attitude, fed by selfishness, can decide that something evil is good. We find this in the mass murder of members of various races and religions.

The Commandments become unbearable burdens that belong to the unenlightened generations of the past or to the people whose needs were small and whose intelligence did not face the demands of human nature. Sin becomes a fact hidden in the history of the past and non-existent in the modern vocabulary. As Pilate asked, "What is truth?" (John 18:38), the world asks "What is sin?" In this way sin becomes an attitude of mind—an offense against one's neighbor at its worst—but never an offense against God.

The world cannot acknowledge that when man offends another man he offends God and when he offends God, he offends his neighbor. The Mystical Body, whose head is Christ, is a tightly knit organism—sensitive to the least pain—rejoicing at the least bit of happiness. One cannot isolate any part of it or separate it from the whole Body.

When a Christian is bombarded with attitudes of pursuing pleasure at any cost, independence from society and alienation from God and the acquisition of money, he must choose between these allurements and goodness, sin and holiness, God and the world.

Jesus reminded us of the desire for worldly possessions when He said, "No servant can be the slave of two masters: he will either hate the first and love the second, or treat the first with respect and the second with scorn. You cannot be the slave of God and money" (Matt. 6:24).

"The Pharisees, who loved money, heard all this and laughed at Him. He said to them, "You are the very ones who pass yourselves off as virtuous in people's sight, but God knows your hearts. For what is thought highly of by men is loathsome in the sight of God" (Luke 16:14-15).

It is a frightening thought to ponder — the things we cling to, covet and pursue as "good," may be an abomination to God. Wealth and the acquisition of worldly power are counted by God as nothing in relation to the kingdom. Unfortunately the possession of these things is something visible, while spiritual riches are invisible. Man is tempted by what he sees, hears, smells, tastes and touches. He is called to higher things by invisible, intangible yearnings, urges from the Supreme Being and knowledge that there is something somewhere better than he sees and feels here in this world. However, unless his Faith is strong, the loud noise of what he hears drowns out the soft voice of God and Conscience. The things he sees ever beckon to him to feast and rest his eyes on the things that pass. It is difficult to push against such tremendous odds, but the gentle breeze of God will quiet the whirling wind of temptation if we cling to what we know is the most perfect way.

THE FLESH

"It is the spirit that gives life, the flesh has nothing to offer" (John 6:63).

Along with outside forces there is within our very being, weaknesses, frailties, inclinations, passions and assorted evil tendencies that make being good seem a far off goal.

We find it easier to be bad than good, angry than gentle, resentful than merciful. Each one of us has some particular weakness that towers over all our other frailties and causes us to fall. Some are proud and find humility and obedience difficult. Some are greedy and find generosity with their time, talent or goods very difficult. Some are cold and indifferent and find loving their neighbor a trying experience. The list of human weaknesses could go on and on but one thing is positive — we must overcome these weaknesses in our souls.

It is in this area we find the cross. We can see and sense outside influences, so our decisions can be clearer, but when our choices between good and evil stem from our own inner being, it is not always clear. Our weaknesses are so much a part of us we are seldom aware of their existence or influence. Our personality is affected by them, making a complete conversion nearly impossible.

Even those who have been blessed by God with sudden conversions or the overcoming of serious weaknesses, find themselves beset with temptations in one area or another and continue to fight against their faults in spite of their conversion.

Perhaps one of the greatest crosses in our lives is to observe the reaction of other people to our personality and weaknesses. We all arouse the faults of others in one way or another and we do this most of the time without knowing or meaning to do so. Friction between various temperaments provides the self-knowledge we all need in order to change. This self-knowledge is not always desirable or accepted and as a result we go through life with neither the light to see ourselves nor the courage to accept ourselves.

We tend to remove ourselves from people and situations that mirror our own souls. No matter where we go we will find ourselves and our weaknesses at work — rising, falling and rising again — meeting those whose friendship somehow brings out the best in us and others whose very presence has the power to draw out the worst in us.

There is in the depths of our being the desire to be good and to be holy, but from that same being rises a cry of rebellion — a spirit of independence that desires to answer to no one. These two spirits challenge each other, fight each other, conquer each other and almost destroy each other in the depths of our souls. There are times we are surprised by the heights of our holy desires and other times horrified by the depths of evil into which we could fall.

St. Paul painted a vivid picture of this state when he said, "I cannot understand my own behavior. I fail to carry out the things I want to do and I find myself doing the very things I hate.... for though the will to do what is good is in me, the performance is not.... every single time I want to do good, it is something evil that comes to hand" (Rom. 7:15, 18, 21). Every day we face our greatest foe—ourselves—and every day God fills us with His grace that we may rise above the things that pull us down and make us forget our dignity as sons of God.

God uses every scrap of our weaknesses and somehow turns them into good. St. Paul assured us of this when he said, "We know that by turning everything to their good, God cooperates with those who love Him" (Rom. 8:28). We need to keep this truth in mind when our human nature seems out to destroy us.

With all our desires to be good and holy there is in our soul that constant struggle between what we are and what we want to be. Why did God leave us with the consequence of original sin after His Divine Son redeemed us and His Spirit gave us a new birth? For some mysterious reason—a reason above our intelligence—God preferred to give us an example of how to overcome rather than take away our frailties. He preferred to have poor weak human beings overcome His archenemy by the power of the Spirit living in them. He thought it more noble to change by free choice than by being free of weaknesses. He wanted us to share the triumph of victory over sin rather than freedom from pain.

He knew our need for Him would be constant as we strove ever so feebly to be good. He saw in that striving tremendous growth, strength, determination and courage—all of which would be lacking without the struggle. He saw the Enemy humiliated by the fruit of virtue winning over the inclination to sin. Although this knowledge is encouraging and helpful to us it is easily forgotten as we struggle on in the battle between vice and virtue.

Sin is painted by the Enemy and the world as something good; our weaknesses are presented to us as just a part of being human. The consequence of this thinking is disastrous. We fail to see the necessity of pain and sacrifice to attain virtue.

We look at God in a spirit of arrogance as if He had no right to ask us to struggle in order to overcome, to suffer in order to change, to fall in order to be humble, to fail in order to be grateful and to be weak in order to do great things.

We do not see our pride because we think we are self-sufficient. We do not see our total dependence on Him because we only see our own strength. We do not see Him as the only source of Goodness because we are so content with our own acts of kindness.

Our weaknesses make us rebel against His Goodness and our goodness makes us attribute virtue to ourselves. We are caught between what we are, what we *think* we are and what He wants us to be.

There are times our weaknesses overpower every semblance of good in us and all seems hopeless. Then suddenly, His grace fills us with strength and light and we rise above ourselves. It is during these times that we can look back and see the fruit God brought forth from our failures and a feeling of assurance fills our souls like the calm after a storm.

God's Will at moments like these is "good" in our eyes. Humility enlightens the mind to see a tiny glimpse of the Wisdom of God. However, it is only a short time before the third Enemy tempts the soul, for he sees progress in holiness and his hatred turns to fury.

THE ENEMY

"Be calm but vigilant, because your Enemy the devil is prowling round like a roaring lion, looking for someone to eat. Stand up to him, strong in faith" (1 Pet. 5:8-9). The words "calm" and "vigilant" describe important attitudes in our fight against this third Tempter in our lives—the devil. Though his presence should be the most obvious, his tactics are so devious and his snares so subtle, many believe he does not exist. However, Jesus, Scripture and daily experience prove otherwise—he exists and is very much alive.

His favorite place of temptation is our Memory and Imagination. The Memory is the only faculty of our soul over which he can have power. This power we ourselves give him in proportion to how much we permit that faculty to be influenced by him. He has no access to our Intellect or Will unless we open the doors to these two faculties to him. He tempts us but we make the choice to permit him entrance to the soul.

This is why Jesus asked us to bless our enemies, do good to those who offend us and forgive seventy times seventy. It is very important that bitterness, rancor, hatred, revenge and depression do not get possession of our Memory. The Enemy's tactics are very subtle in this area, in fact almost imperceptible. He makes us feel we always have a legitimate excuse for hating or not forgiving. Our feelings of revenge or bitterness look so just and right that these feelings become imbedded in our very being. They can become so much a part of us that we do not recognize them for what they are—dangerous attitudes designed by the Enemy to destroy us—inspired by the Enemy to mold our souls into his image—an image of hate and confusion.

We are not always conscious of his influence because our feelings are being nourished by what the Enemy considers Truth, but we must remember the "truth is not in him" (John 8:44). When we are offended he brings out the evident fact of that offense and makes us feel perfectly justified in our resentment and pride. So much so that we quote Scripture to substantiate our feelings. We find those who are resentful and revengeful quoting "an eye for an eye and a tooth for a tooth" (Exod. 21:24). Those who have moral problems quote Our Lord's merciful treatment of the woman taken in adultery. "Has no one condemned you?... Neither do I condemn you" (John 8:10-11). Drunkards excuse their bad habits by reminding everyone that Jesus and His disciples drank wine. Those who indulge in frequent bouts of anger quote the passage showing Jesus making a whip and driving out the money changers from the Temple. We look and the Enemy makes us find whatever Scripture passage, excuse, or reason we need for harboring evil in our hearts. He wants our bitterness to appear as natural as possible—only a part of being human—and then slowly the venom of evil takes possession of our hearts and we become blind to all goodness.

Perhaps one of the greatest temptations of the Enemy is lethargy and a feeling of complacency. This lazy, self-satisfied attitude can destroy our souls faster than more obvious temptations. Big weaknesses that attract the attention of others are often overcome by human respect. We are humiliated when others see our true self and we put forth more effort to overcome. But spiritual lethargy is not as noticeable and is hidden under the guise of being too busy to pray and totally convinced we are exerting our utmost for the kingdom.

We tell ourselves and others that we are doing our very best and nothing else is required. This is the very attitude the Pharisee had in the Temple. He was perfectly satisfied with himself and his efforts to glorify God. There was no question in his mind that in the order of merit he was on top. Jesus condemned his attitude and told the shocked crowd, listening to this account, that the man went away satisfied with himself but displeasing to the Father (Luke 18:11-14).

The Publican in the back of the Temple, who was unhappy with himself, acknowledging his inadequacy and realizing there was much to be done, went away pleasing to God. He saw himself, admitted his sinner condition, asked God for help and went away looking forward to the future, not backward to what was accomplished. He would not rest in the past as the Pharisee did. He would change and depend upon the mercy of God to uphold him.

The great deception in the Pharisee's conduct was the appearance of good—good conduct, good works, good morals. We must keep in mind that here, deep in the recesses of the soul, self-satisfaction had long ruled as Master. Good deeds were accomplished for the sake of self-glory, not the glory of God. God was merely an onlooker who somehow should be grateful to the Pharisee for being so generous.

When we act as if we were the source of our talents and accomplishments, we can be sure the "father of lies" (John 8:44) has accomplished his work. However, complacency is not the only temptation the Enemy places in our path. There are thoughts of envy over another's goods, jealousy over another's talents, gluttony in taste and inordinate attachment to things and people. Yes, love itself can be used against us. We can love someone so much that life and happiness depend upon that person. Fear and insecurity can grip a soul in that condition and deprive it of any joy or peace. Life becomes a nightmare whenever our lives are wrapped up in the things that change and pass away.

The Enemy makes us feel there is more security in the visible than the invisible, more love in what feels good than in the cross that is disagreeable. He turns and twists everything around and away from God, enhances the need for pleasure and increases our disgust for the cross. He whispers in our ear that this world is all there is so he can deprive us of possessing the place he lost in the kingdom.

It is easy to see that his disguises are so well planned we run the risk of not recognizing him at all and this is without doubt his most clever tool. Only death will tear off his mask and show us his influence in our lives. We must pray and ask the Spirit within us to give us discernment now—in this life—so we may ever be aware of his disguises and deceptions.

We must "make our home" (John 14:23) in Jesus, whose Presence in our souls surrounds us with a protective shield against the hatred of the Enemy. We will become sensitive to his temptations and see his actions clearly. With this perception we will be able to make the right choices and bear good fruit, "fruit that lasts" (John 15:16).

Reaction to His Will

The angels must look upon us with astonishment as we question and rebel against God's Will in our lives. Perhaps a good comparison for our attitudes in this regard is to imagine an ant looking up at a giant and saying, "I can see more than you see. I know more than you know and I can do more than you can do." The thought of such a scene brings laughter to our hearts and a sense of the ridiculous. But is it? How many of us are not guilty of just such an action as we complain and rebel against God's Will?

What we are really saying to God in our rebellion is that we know better than He does the things that are for our happiness in this life and necessary for our salvation. There is hardly a cross we accept with Hope, knowing it is for our good. Nor do we accept pain or tragedy, understanding that His love will bring good out of it.

We are consistent in our insistence that we are always right and He is wrong. However, we find no trouble in accepting the opinions of those with a higher degree of intelligence than our own. We trust a surgeon with our life because he understands our illness and is able to heal it. We trust the opinions and facts presented to us by scientists concerning planets, stars, atoms, medicine and electronics. We do this without the least comprehension on our part of what they say or mean. We only know they are experts in a particular field beyond our intelligence or education, so our trust is complete. Isn't it strange that we do not give God the same courtesy?

There is a difference between not understanding God's Will and questioning God's Will. We see this clearly in the Gospel narrative of Mary and Zechariah. Zechariah, hearing from the angel that his wife would bear a son, questioned God's Will and said, "How can I be sure of this? I am an old man and my wife is getting on in years" (Luke 1:18-34). The whole thing seemed impossible to Zechariah and he could not see the possibility of such a miracle. Everything seemed against it. He questioned God's power and wisdom. Mary, however only wondered how

God would fulfill the message He had given her. She asked for direction. There was no question in her heart, only how she could fulfill His wishes.

We see here that our lack of ability to comprehend God's Will is an act of humility on our part, but our questioning the wisdom of His Will is pride. The former says, "My mind is too small to see beyond my own little world, but I will do Your Will because I know You desire only what is for my good." The latter says, "Why did You let this happen? This is not just; this is not fair. My way would have been better; why didn't You answer my prayers?" This is the ant correcting the giant!

God is not displeased if we find it hard to accomplish His Will even when we understand it. We see this example in Matthew. "A man had two sons," Jesus said. "He went and said to the first, 'My boy, you go and work in the vineyard today.' He answered, 'I will not go' but afterwards thought better of it and went. The man then said the same thing to the second son who answered, 'Certainly, sir,' but did not go. Which of the two did the father's will? 'The first they said" (Matt. 21:28-31). When Jesus told us the first son "thought better of it" He was telling us the son's first impulse was to rebel—to say no, but the more he thought about the request, the more his conscience bothered him. Repentance and love for his father made him do the father's will. So it is with us. Our first reaction to God's Will is often a flat "no." This surface "no" is not deep rooted and our loving Father understands. Our merit is enhanced when we find His Will difficult and still accomplish it.

Love makes us conform to God's Will but it doesn't always make it easy. This was so with Jesus Himself in the Garden of Gethsemane. "My Father," He said, "if it is possible, let this cup pass me by. Nevertheless, let it be as You, not I, would have it" (Matt. 26:39). Three times He repeated the same words and three times there was silence. There are no words recorded between the Father and Jesus. We find no dialogue—no yes or no—no explanation—only silence. But that silence spoke volumes to Jesus. It meant, "Go on—it must be this way. Redemption can be accomplished no better way." Jesus did not rebel against the silence—He accepted it with love and determination.

Though Jesus has given us an example, we still do not heed His call to imitation. God's silence to our prayers for help infuriates us and we take that silence as an act of punishment on God's part. We do not take the time to pray as Jesus did—"pray the longer" for knowledge and strength to accomplish the Divine plan. Just as an angel came from heaven to give Jesus strength, so in the hours of our fear and distress, God's own Spirit will give us the fortitude we need (Luke 22:43). But we must have that humble heart so necessary to admit that at this moment we do not know what is best for us—only God knows that hidden mystery.

Desiring His Will

As we have looked at what our usual reaction to God's Will is, let us look at what Jesus expects it to be. When the Apostles urged Jesus to eat near the well of Samaria, He refused their food and said, "I have a food that you do not know about." So the disciples asked one another, "Has someone been bringing him food?" But Jesus said, "My food is to do the Will of the One who sent me and to complete His work" (John 4:32-34).

The necessity for food implies hunger—a longing for nourishment—a sustenance that promotes strength, energy and growth. This is exactly what God's Will does in our lives.

God's Will is to our soul what food is to our body. It promotes growth in holiness, strength for daily trials, strength to carry the cross and zeal to persevere in our desire for God.

As natural food loses its own identity and is changed into our body with its various organs and functions, so God's Will, as it is united to ours, changes us into living images of His Son. As the seed planted in the ground dies before it grows and bears fruit, so our Will must die to its own desires and bury itself in the Divine Will. Like food it will lose its own identity and become one with God.

This desire to do God's Will must be more than the acceptance of the inevitable. It must be a seeking, finding, uniting experience. "My aim," Jesus told His Apostles, "is to do not my own Will but the Will of Him who sent me" (John 5:30). And when He taught His disciples how to pray He inserted the petition that we be given the grace to accomplish His "Will on earth in the same way it is in heaven" (Matt. 6:10).

The one goal of every Christian is to know and accomplish God's Will and in the same way it is done in heaven—with obedience, promptness and love. We are speaking here of love of preference—meaning we prefer God's Will over our own, whether or not it is difficult or to our liking.

A union of Sonship is established between God and the soul when the two wills become one. This is why Jesus told the crowds one day that His Mother was precious to the Father more because she conformed perfectly to His Will, than by the privilege of being the Mother of His Son. "Who are my mother and my brothers?" (Matt. 12:48). And looking around at those sitting in a circle about him, he said, "Here are my mother and my brothers. Anyone who does the Will of God, that person is my brother and sister and mother" (Mark 3:33-35).

Such a reward for conforming to a perfect Will is beyond our imagination. This privilege is for every Christian. We need not envy the Apostles, for our opportunities are as great as theirs. The difference between us and those first followers of Jesus lies not in a lack of opportunities or grace, but in a lack of union with God's Will.

The purpose of our existence is to become a clear image of Jesus by the perfect conformity of our Will to God. Jesus told us, "I have come from heaven not to do my own Will but to do the Will of the One who sent me" (John 6:38). We see Jesus saying over and over that His one goal was to do the Father's Will.

God has given us the gift of free will for the purpose of freely choosing Him above ourselves. It is a matter of prefer-ence—a matter of love. Love motivates our Will either in the direction of God or ourselves. The successful man is not the one who makes a million dollars, but the one who succeeds in uniting his Will to God. Without God, the successful man may be a slave to his own whims, society and the world while the man whose Will ever lives in God is free.

Knowing God's Will

The difficulty most of us experience is not so much in doing God's Will as in simply knowing what that Will is for us. In this regard there are some things we are positive are God's Will, for example: The Commandments—the Ten as given to Moses, the Precepts of the Church, the duties of our state of life, obedience to lawful authority—civil, family and church, and the New Commandment as given by Jesus, to love one another.

In the Gospels we see in many simple ways exactly what the Father expects of us. These are all direct manifestations of the Will of God in our daily lives. Perhaps a list of some of these positive commandments may be of help.

1. "Love your enemies, do good to those who hate you, bless those who curse you, pray for those who treat you badly" (Luke 6:27-28).

2. Be compassionate as your Father is compassionate. Do not judge and you will not be judged; do not condemn and you will not be condemned" (Luke 6:36-37).

3. "I tell you solemnly, anyone who does not welcome the Kingdom of God like a little child will never enter it" (Luke 18:17).

4. "It is my Father's will that whoever sees the Son and believes in him shall have eternal life" (John 6:40).

5. "Shoulder my yoke and learn from me for I am gentle and humble of heart" (Matt. 11:29).

6. "Before the world was made, he chose us, chose us in Christ to be holy and spotless, and to live through love in His Presence" (Eph. 1:4).

7. "What God wants is for you all to be holy" (1 Thess. 4:2-3).

Our problem may be that we look upon the Commandments in a rather negative way. They are for the most part "don't" directives in our minds but this is not so. We do not find fault with the inventor of a machine when he gives us directions on how to obtain the best results from what he invented. Who else would know how best a particular machine runs than its inventor! To most of us this is logical and we are willing to follow directions and accept the fact that most equipment is only guaranteed providing directions are properly followed.

This is exactly what God has done in giving us Commandments. They are not the demands of a Creator who makes His creatures ever aware of their subordinate position. The Commandments, given by the Father in the Old and by Jesus in the New Testament, are only directions that say Human Beings He created are happier, healthier and more content when they follow the directions of their Creator.

The Father knows under what conditions our souls grow and mature. He knows what remedies are best for their weaknesses. He knows what steps must be taken to avoid the many obstacles the Enemy strews in our path. Most of all, He knows in what way our souls need to be purified, tempered and transformed so they can one day stand in His awesome Presence and not be annihilated.

The Scriptures are full of revelations telling how the Father wishes us to think and act under every circumstance. Our problem in knowing God's Will then is in the decisions we make in our daily lives. First, it must be said the Commandments mentioned above are part of God's Ordaining Will. There is no question here of what He wants. But the trials of daily life, the evil, suffering, etc. are part of God's Permitting Will.

God's Ordaining Will wants only what is good and holy, but man's free will and the temptations of the Enemy produce other effects that are not good. These effects we suffer from, but God, to whom all things are present, sees some good in our endurance of pain and evil and for the sake of a greater good, He permits evil.

St. Paul brought this out when he reminded us that to those who love God all things tend to good (Rom. 8:28). Our dear Lord endured the malice, hatred and finally crucifixion to accomplish God's Will.

We cannot say God ordained that men reject and kill His Son, but knowing beforehand the sentiments of the Chosen People towards His Son's appearance on earth, He *permitted* their evil dispositions and by His Son's perfect *acceptance* of these evils, He wrought our Redemption. He ordained that man not fall, but pride rejected that desire. He ordained that man accept His Son, but many did not. In permitting the effects of non-acceptance, the Father saw great good. Man would forever know how much he was loved by God. He would be the recipient of the Spirit, grace, Divine Sonship and finally heaven. All this good was wrapped securely behind the malice of men. God saw it and permitted His Son to suffer grievously in order to break the hold of the Enemy upon mankind and finally destroy death completely by a glorious Resurrection.

The Father has that same love for us and our Faith, Hope and Love must ever burn brightly as we endure the trials He permits in our lives. Trust is the key to accomplishing God's Will. We must trust the Father whose Eyes are ever ahead of us. We cannot see or judge our way in a dense fog, but we can have trust in the Father, who sees all things ahead clearly.

In making our decisions as to a state in life, friends, work, future plans, business ventures, etc. we must first arrive at some guidelines, use the mental faculties God has already given us and pray for guidance. We cannot expect Him to come down in some ecstatic vision and tell us exactly what to do.

Perhaps some guidelines would be to see if the decision we need to make is for the greater honor and glory of God, how does it affect our relationship with Him and are we at peace with it. We can rest assured that if we make our decisions in this light, God will stand by us and bring good out of it even if we see later our decisions were not the most perfect.

Failure is also used by God to bring us closer to Him. He never commanded us to always make the right decisions—only to be holy and that entails a childlike confidence that He will make our crooked ways straight and our faltering steps firm.

When we have an occasion to change friends we already have a criterion to go by. Jesus told us to judge by fruits. Our friends must be chosen not only by the fruit they bear in their own lives but by the fruit we bear in their company. We can arrive at some concept of God's Will in relationship to work by the talents God has given us. What kind of work am I happy doing? If we are not sure, we need to experiment with various types of work until we arrive at that "at home" awareness that this is what we can do best.

It happens, however, that sometimes we live in a particular situation that was brought about by our own weakness, mistakes, wrong decisions and the evil intentions of our neighbor. Where is God's Will in this? If we have prayed and no solution is at hand, if we try to change the matter and things only get worse, we can be sure that patient endurance is God's Will, at least for the moment. Continuous prayer will bring fortitude and fortitude will bring perseverance, perseverance will bring Hope and that Hope will not be in vain.

St. Paul told the Corinthians, "We are in difficulties on all sides, but never cornered; we see no answer to our problems, but never despair" (2 Cor. 4:8). Even a holy, specially chosen soul such as Paul had moments when God's will was not clear—when everything seemed impossible. This is why one day Paul besought the Lord to relieve him of his multitudinous problems. He began to think God's Will was not in his trials, weaknesses, insults, hardships, persecutions and the agonies of the Apostolate (2 Cor. 12:8-10). So it was that three times he asked for relief and the reply he received reassured him that if it was happening, God's Will would bring good out of it. "My grace," Jesus answered Paul, "is enough for you; my power is at its best in weakness" (2 Cor. 12:9). Paul rejoiced at this. It did not lessen his sorrows, but the knowledge that God's grace was with him made him say, "I shall be very happy to make my weaknesses my special boast so that the power of Christ may stay over me" (2 Cor. 12:9).

This is the difference between a pagan and a Christian. To a pagan there is no purpose to suffering. As a result, he lives a life of loneliness and frustration. The Christian may be experiencing much the same trials as the pagan and never lose his joy. He sees God's will in it, sees an opportunity to be like Jesus, and sees greater glory in the kingdom. The pagan's trials are increased by despair and the Christian's lightened by sharing the yoke of Jesus.

Many ask the question, "How do I know this is God's Will for me?" The answer is simply, "If it is happening, it is God's Will." Nothing happens to us that He has not seen beforehand, pondered the good we would derive and put upon it His stamp of approval.

God's Will is manifested to us in the duties and experiences of the present moment. We have only to accept them and try to be like Jesus in them. When Jesus made no answer to Pilate, Pilate said to Him, "Are you refusing to speak to me? Surely, you know I have power to release you and I have power to crucify you" (John 19:10). The reply Jesus made shows us very clearly that Jesus saw the Father's Will in every moment to moment experience, just or unjust. "You would have no power over me, if it had not been given you from above" (John 19:11). Jesus saw the Father in a weak, unjust judge. How many of us have that kind of confidence—that kind of insight!

St. Peter encouraged the Christians of his day to "accept the authority of every social institution; the emperor as the supreme authority and the governors.... God wants us to be good citizens.... have respect for everyone.... and honor the emperor" (1 Pet. 2:13-17). We are all aware of the fact that Peter was speaking here of Nero, whose wickedness is well known. However, it goes without saying that if lawful authority demands a rejection of God or God's Commandments, we must choose God before all else.

God did not redeem us in order to place us in some kind of earthly Utopia. He redeemed us to give us a kingdom, to make us adopted sons, to give us everlasting joy, to witness to the world the existence of another life and to prove by our personal conversion that Jesus is the Son of God.

St. Paul assures us that all the suffering in the world is not worthy to be compared with the glory that is to come (Rom. 8:18).

Every moment of life is like a sacrament in which we can receive God. It is a channel through which God speaks to us, forms us and directs us. We have only to accept the duties of the present moment to find God's Will. We are hampered in breathing this supernatural air by the fact we see only people and circumstances, brought about by the malice or temperaments of others. They become obstacles in our path and prevent us from seeing God.

We cannot see God *in* their actions because these actions are opposed to His Ordaining Will. However, we can see God *through* these actions, like seeing a beloved friend through a dense fog. In that fog we may still stumble and fall, cry and despair at times, but that Figure ever beckons us forward to a greater light beyond.

The secret then in finding God's Will is to see Him in the present moment and react to that Presence in as loving a way as we can. It takes a little effort to see God in everything, but Jesus did just that and His complete obedience won our salvation.

There are times when we need to make "on the spot" decisions—occasions when there is hardly time for a prayer. In these circumstances we can be sure that if our heart has been with God up to that moment, we will make the correct move. If we fail, our hope in His Love assures us He will bring good out of it.

God does not want us to fret and worry about yesterday or tomorrow. We read in St. Matthew's Gospel that Jesus said, "Do not worry about tomorrow; tomorrow will take care of itself. Each day has enough trouble of its own" (Matt. 6:34). Here is a call from Jesus to live in the present moment. Jesus is not telling us that as Christians we will be trouble free. He is telling us to bear our yoke with Him and do it on a moment to moment basis. If we exercise ourselves in this kind of living, we will have the presence of mind to see His Will and the strength to do it.

There is no blueprint—no certain way of knowing the Will of God in our material decisions. Our God-given intellect and the discernment of His Spirit living in our hearts, will give us the necessary tools to make better than average correct decisions. Sometimes His permitting Will allows our failures to exercise our Faith, increase our Hope and cause us to cling to Him as our Friend in need.

There will be times His Will is so cloudy in our minds and the path so uncertain, that we are forced to choose the least doubtful path and hope for the best. All our peace in these circumstances comes from the deep realization, still alive among dying embers, that God is our Father and He will take care of us.

God is not the tyrant we find the world to be. He is satisfied with sincere effort to know and accomplish His Will. He will crown these efforts with success though all seems lost.

Living in His Will

The first step in our efforts to glorify God is to *know* God's will. The second step, however, is the most important and that is: how do we live in that Will—how do we fulfill it—how do we accomplish that Will with joy?

To do this we must look at the life of Jesus. Jesus saw in every facet of His life, the Will of His Father. He seemed preoccupied with it. When He spoke, He told the crowds the words He spoke were the Father's words. When He healed, He told them He only did the "work" of the Father. When He was in pain, He saw the love of the Father for mankind permitting Him to suffer in order to redeem us.

Perhaps the most helpful comment Jesus made about the Father's Will was when He said it was His food. Though each person's state in life is different, each one's work and mission are different, the one common goal we should all desire is that of living in His Will—not just accomplishing it—but, like Jesus, living in it. It should be the food and nourishment of our souls.

Jesus saw the Father in everything. When trials and heartaches came His way He saw opportunities to offer a pleasing sacrifice to the Father. He also saw the opportunity to confound the Enemy of His Father.

Every time the Pharisees embarrassed Him in front of the crowds, He practiced some virtue to an heroic degree. Opportunities that the Enemy provoked which would ordinarily call forth anger, hatred and resentment in most of us, Jesus reacted to in the opposite way. His reactions would be silent or gentle. Even the few times He lashed out at the Pharisees and called them hypocrites, He did so with the intention of enlightening the people and pricking the consciences of those who had strayed from the path of integrity.

Every moment of life gave Jesus opportunities to act as man in a God-like way. He paved the way for each one of us to use the gifts of the present moment in a God-like fashion. He merited His Spirit to live in our souls so we would be able to do the same things He did.

His whole life on earth spoke of living in the Father's will in a hundred different ways. The Father was constantly calling forth in Jesus some facet of His own perfections—perfections visible for us to see, admire and imitate.

We see in Jesus the Father's Mercy as He forgave sinners, the Father's compassion as He healed the sick, the Father's patience as He explained exalted mysteries in simple parables.

This same reflection must be seen in us. Our desire as Christians should be to act as much like Jesus as the light and grace of the present moment permit. That light and grace will vary from moment to moment and grow from day to day. As we are patient with our neighbor, we must be patient with ourselves because God is patient with us. He knows how difficult it is for us to live in His Will. He accepts our feeble efforts to obey, our grumbling moments of rebellion and our vacillating spirit. He knows that the more we grow in love, the more detached we will be from our own will. The more we love the Father, the more we will accomplish His Will.

There is a bittersweet side of love that we cannot overlook. Love is only proven by a willingness to sacrifice — to give of ourselves. This is true of natural and supernatural love. A mother, who refuses to care for a sick child, loves little. The worry, anxiety and care of a loving mother proves her love for her children. The Father's love for us was manifested when His desire to have us with Him in the kingdom, compelled Him to send His own Son to redeem us. It was an act of love that commanded the Eternal Word to become man. It was another act of love that responded with a never to be forgotten, "I go to do Thy Will."

Life should not be a battle of Wills—His and mine. Life is a never ending call to love and an opportunity to respond with the same love—a call to sacrifice our dearest possession just as the Father sacrificed His dearest possession—an opportunity to say, "I love you, Father, more than myself."

Love then, is the axis on which the Will revolves. If our love is selfish, our Will is geared toward self-gratification. If our love is unselfish, our Will is directed toward the Glory of God and the good of our neighbor.

We cannot separate love from the Will, for love decides what direction the Will takes. Even those who reject God possess a kind of love—a love for evil—evil deeds—evil company. Eventually, an eternal hatred is born from this love for evil. Pride is a misdirected love and if unconquered during life, turns inward with such force, its back is turned away from God forever. This is the great sin which is difficult to repent of: not admitting error and not accepting dependence on God.

It is important that we be vigilant as to the direction our love takes, for we will find love and the Will, side by side in everything we do. This is why Jesus constantly urged us to do the Father's Will. It was like saying "Love my Father with all your heart, soul and mind" (Mark 12:30). Be ready to manifest that love by doing everything to please Him — to do His Will — to prefer His Will and love to your own love and to your own Will.

Love is proven, not by how much we know about God or how long we pray. It is proven by the degree of union of our will with the Will of God. It does not matter if the accomplishing of that Will is difficult. Jesus prayed long in the Garden of Olives, because the Father's Will at that moment was difficult. His love was proven by the calm and ready acceptance of the Father's negative reply to His appeal.

In our daily lives it is not possible to like everything that happens to us. However, it is possible to see the loving hand of God, directing and redirecting every facet of our lives. It soon becomes a joy to see how He manages to bring good out of our mistakes and make right our wrong choices.

Every day of our lives should be lived in an attitude of loving expectation and vigilant anticipation of His inspirations, directions, warnings and lights. We were created to fit perfectly into the image of Jesus imprinted upon our souls. That image was made brighter in Baptism and grows clearer by all the sacraments, prayers and good works we participate in. All these aids are given us for the purpose of developing, guiding and directing our will toward God.

A will that is constantly fed by the Word of God in Scripture, the presence of the Spirit in the Church and the presence of Jesus in the Eucharist, will be attracted to the accomplishment of God's Will like a magnet. It will be drawn to God like an irresistible force. It is in a state of continual growth and preparation for the time when there will no longer be Two Wills—His *and* Mine, but only One Will—His *in* Mine.

In the Shadow of His Light

Detachment

I wonder if the best way to become detached is to have an overwhelming attachment to God.

It is not so much the possession of things that makes me attached; it is the burden these things impose — the fear of loss, the greed for more, the power they exert, the glitter that is so bright for so short a time. All of this puts me in a vicious circle that is hard to change. The more I have, the more I want; the more I want, the more anxious I become, and every day my mind and soul are absorbed in a complex web too tight to break through.

The visible reality brings a degree of happiness, but not peace; it gives a glow but not a light; it gives security but never assurance; it promotes love based on service, but never feeds the love that is based on sacrifice.

Is detachment the answer to freedom? I think not, for detachment is negative — it is to be without. The answer must be positive — I must replace what I have with something better. The things that occupy my mind and are contrary to the Divine Will are the things that exercise the greatest power over my soul.

I must rise above the things that pass, by seeing God in them.

The essence of attachment is to possess, to hang on to. And yet, everything is passing. Why should I put my heart in anything that is here today and gone tomorrow.

Where, my soul, is the balance between compassion and detachment, providing for today and not being anxious for tomorrow, having things and not possessing them, deeply caring and being unselfish? The balance is a deep and strong love for God. All lesser loves fade away in the presence of a great Love — and here is the balance and the answer to detachment: Supernatural Love.

Supernatural Love is free and unattached because it is based on an unseen Reality; it is sure because that Reality is eternal; it is strong because it is fed by God Himself; it can possess things without being possessed by them; it can love people and be content if that love is not returned; it can give and give and never run dry.

It is, then, a matter of preference, and of priorities, and first things first. It is not a matter of having or not having, of being rich or poor, a success or a failure. It is putting God and His Kingdom *first*, *foremost* and *always*, and knowing that all these other things will be added.

The secret to real freedom is to prefer God to everything and to do everything for God.

PRAYER

Eternal Father, Your Son Jesus was detached, and yet He loved to the end; He cared and yet was untouched by selfishness; His only desire was to fulfill Your Will, yet He was so thoughtful of the needs of others. Give me the light to see and the courage to let go of the many things in my life that keep me in a constant whirlwind and a vicious circle. Amen.

Jesus Proves His Love

Christ began our Redemption at the Incarnation and culminated it on Calvary, so I must look at the whole Christ.

Everything He did during His life, He did for me, for my direction and instruction. He is Lord, Master, Teacher, and Friend.

Everything He suffered, then, was a witness to His Personal Love for me. I will look at His Hidden Sufferings and learn how to act in my daily life.

JESUS' HIDDEN SUFFERINGS

The intellectuals of His day who were constantly trying to embarrass Him.

The importunity of the crowds that pressed upon Him day and night for cures.

The humiliation of knowing so much and being taught by those who knew so little.

The necessity of running away from enemies.

The fatigue at the end of a hard, tension-filled day.

Knowing the thoughts of those listening to His message.

The suspicion of His relatives who thought He was mad.

The criticism of the priests because He ate and drank with sinners.

The heartache of seeing those in authority disbelieve in His message and Sonship.

His disciples' lack of comprehension of even the simplest parable.

His dependence upon others to provide for His every need.

The jealousy of those who called Him a devil.

The denial of the one He chose to be a leader.

The betrayal of a friend whom He chose to do great things for the Kingdom.

The hardships of hunger, thirst, and no place to lay His head.

Watching many walk away because they found His message "a hard saying."

Knowing that many ran after Him because He fed them, not because they loved Him.

Being abandoned by all His disciples except one.

Knowing that He would be the cause of dissension and would set father against son and brother against brother.

PRAYER

O Jesus, I often experience these kinds of sufferings in my daily life. Give me the serenity You possessed to accept these painful experiences with love. Amen.

God's Love for Me

Before God created a blade of grass, a star, a planet, or an angel, He knew me and loved me. It was then that He decided to create me in this time in history and in this place. How many creatures He could have created and didn't create. He really wanted me to be. I have a particular kind of love and way of loving that He desires me to give Him, and my personality, transformed into Christ, will render a particular kind of love and glory to the Father for all eternity. I am important to God and to the whole world.

God knows me and loves me as an individual. He loves me just as truly and intimately as though no other creature existed.

He loves me no less because He loves millions and millions of other people.

Jesus loves me with a love that is indescribable and inconceivable. There is no language that can express His love.

No imagination can picture His love, no poet describe it, no heart — no matter how loving — can encompass Jesus' love for me.

God loves me because He wants to. His love is free. He patiently waits for the least expression of love on my part.

The Omnipotence of God looks upon my little soul with great tenderness, mercy, and love.

His love for me is steadfast and sure. Though all forsake me and I lose everything, God will always be with me.

If, throughout all creation, God possessed no other creature but myself, He would love me neither more nor less than at this moment.

When I call to mind the myriads of creatures in the world, the millions of stars, planets, and galaxies, the highest Seraphim in the spiritual hierarchy, and realize that not a movement escapes His eye—I am filled with awe that this great God loves me.

The ever-present, Loving God knows my thoughts, desires, and secret aspirations. He understands me perfectly, and this realization gives me joy.

God puts His arms around me as a mother fondles a child. He awaits my every sigh, my every act of love.

Jesus rejoices every time I say, "Jesus, I love You."

He lovingly waits for me to give Him a thought, to unite my will to His Will, and to prefer Him to things.

God created me because He wanted to share His happiness and His love with me. He has waited thousands of millions of years for me to know Him, and in knowing Him to love Him, and in loving Him to prefer Him to all things.

He created me, not through any necessity or advantage on His part, but only out of pure love.

This Infinite God, who stretched out the heavens and laid out the earth, lavishes His love on me.

The Providence of God

If I put a tiny drop of water under a microscope, a whole new world is open to my eyes. Thousands of little things are rushing back and forth, and yet — not one of these little creatures is forgotten by God. If I could see the atomic structure of one cubic inch of wood, I would see trillions of atoms made up of electrons, protons, and neutrons — and yet, God never loses sight of one of these atoms. His watchfulness over me is greater than all these transitory things.

His Providence watches over me with a deep concern in every facet of my life.

He asks me to first seek the Kingdom and He will take care of everything else.

His Son, Jesus, said that the Father knows every sparrow that falls and I am worth more than many sparrows.

The Father knows what I would do in every possible circumstance and state in life, and He directed me to the one I chose, as the one best suited to my salvation.

His love provides or permits people and things to prune my soul of everything that is not like Christ.

He comforts me in times of sorrow with the comforting words of a neighbor, the smile of a child, or the love of a friend.

Divine Providence disposes and directs everything to one end: the glory of God. Nothing happens by chance or without reason. It is all, without exception, a part of an overall plan of God.

In God's plan, I have a definite place, and I must contribute to the good of all.

I cannot see the reason for pain, suffering, heartache, or disappointment, but this is only because I do not see the whole plan and how each incident fits in like a thread in a beautiful tapestry.

The Goodness of God is completely trustworthy, for His Wisdom "reaches from end to end mightily, and orders all things sweetly" (Wisd. 8:1, Douay-Rheims).

Divine Providence addresses these words to me, "Can a woman forget her infant.... And if she should forget, yet will I not forget thee" (Isa. 49:15, Douay-Rheims).

It is discouraging at times when in spite of real effort on my part I fall again and again. I must realize that His Providence is with me and He is teaching me humility. He wants me to rise after each fall with greater confidence and to understand that saints are holy not because they never fell but because they rose promptly and trusted in His Mercy and Love.

Divine Providence uses illness, separations, misunderstandings, failures, and abandonment by friends, to purify my soul and to detach me from temporal things.

God uses the ill will, hatred, and defects of people to purify my self-love and humble my pride. It is necessary that I see His hand in everything and not only the imperfections of my neighbor in my regard.

The Good God, who is so lavish in His care of nature, looks after me with much more love and attention. He wants me to share in His Providence by working and exerting my own effort to provide food and shelter, but He does not want me to be anxious for tomorrow. "His Providence rises before the dawn."

PRAYER

O God, help me to be Poor in Spirit and place all my trust in You. I ask for courage not to be excessively solicitous for my daily needs because I know I am worth more than many sparrows and You take care of me. Amen.

The Lowest Place

The word "humility" is misunderstood by most people and despised by others. It is not making oneself a door mat. Jesus told us to learn from Him how to be meek and humble of heart. I must look at His life if I am to have any concept of what humility is all about.

Christ took the form of a servant but He never ceased to be the Master; He took the lowest place but was always the Leader; He was meek when accused unjustly, but strong enough to call men hypocrites when He had to; He cured the blind and then told them not to tell anyone; He was lowly in appearance but never lost His dignity; He felt the jealousy and hatred of His enemies but never lost His serenity; He said that without Him I could do nothing, yet He gave credit to the Father for everything He did; He was afraid in the Garden of

Gethsemane, but did what He had to do; He suffered unheard of torments and asked forgiveness for His executioners; He felt abandoned but commended His soul to His Father. This is how He was humble.

Humility is to know my place before God and to be grateful and take my place before men with lowliness.

Self-Control

When the Master said I should carry my cross and follow Him —and unless I died to self I would not find life—what did he mean? When I deny myself, what am I really doing? I must answer these questions if I am to bear the fruit of self-control.

The power of my will is so strong that I can say "no" even to God. Although it is a spiritual faculty, it needs exercise in order to strengthen itself—just as a muscle needs exercise to keep its tone. Misuse and no use mean death to both physical and spiritual faculties. If I am going to have the courage to do God's Will in big things, I must strengthen my will in little things. Every time I say "no" to a small temptation, I strengthen my will to say "no" in greater ones.

Without mortification I am a slave to myself and unable to say "no" to any desire or whim. I am truly in bondage. I am cast to and fro by everything and everyone, and because I roll with the tide I am under the impression all is well and I am in control. It is only when I am dashed against the rocks of disillusion and desolation, alone and bitter, that the awful truth hits home: I am a slave to my own will.

How necessary it is for me to deny myself in small things in order to give to my soul strength of character and stability.

The more my will is turned toward God, the greater will be my union with His Son.

Positive Effects of Self-Denial

Love is increased when I refrain from speaking of my neighbor's faults.

Patience grows when I listen to a boring account of a friend's neurosis.

Temperance becomes stronger when I use moderation.

Justice is sweetened when I put myself in my neighbor's shoes and forgive his offenses.

Gentleness gives me more control when the opportunity to lose my temper is squelched.

Humility is preserved when I give credit where credit is due — to God.

Prudence becomes easy when I forget myself and look for the good of others.

Fortitude is strengthened when I accept pain and suffering with resignation.

Joy increases when it is dependent upon doing God's Will and not mine. And so it is with every virtue. The more I strengthen my will by self-denial, the greater is my self-control. Peace of soul is preserved, and the reflection of Jesus grows brighter and brighter.

The Call to Holiness

I am called by God to become holy with a holiness similar to His own: "Be holy as your Heavenly Father is holy" (Matt. 5:48) — and "This is the will of God — your sanctification" (1 Thess. 4:3).

I wonder if I understand what it means to be called to holiness? God alone is holy and good and I find myself in the same position as St. Paul when he said that the things he wanted to do, he did not do, and the things he didn't want to do, he did.

This proves that Paul was an ordinary man with a mission from God. I, too, have a mission. It may not be a public one as his was, but it is a mission nonetheless.

My mission is to cooperate with the working of the Holy Spirit in my life by developing the seed of holiness (grace), planted in my soul at Baptism.

This seed is capable of bearing beautiful fruits of holiness, and will help build up the Body of Christ in His Church and in His people. The essence of holiness is not doing great things, but in doing ordinary things with great love for God and neighbor.

I must pattern my life by the Lord Jesus and not by my neighbor's life or my own concept of perfection.

A preconceived idea of holiness can hamper my soul and prevent me from following the inspirations of the Holy Spirit. My type of sanctity may be totally different from anyone else's, so I must be pliable in the Lord's hands and let Him mold me according to His designs and my personality.

The seeds the Spirit sows in my soul are my seeds, not someone else's, and only when the storms of life have watered, the sun of love fed, and the hand of God pruned, will these seeds spring up and bear fruit for others to see and be nourished.

I must not be concerned with what kind of fruit I will bear, or how much; the fruit is the Lord's. I must only make sure there is plenty of food and water.

The common denominator between the rich and poor, young and old, sick and healthy, strong and weak, is *love*. God is Love, and the more there is of God in me, the holier I will become, and the more like Him will I be in all my actions. My whole being will be transformed into Jesus: His thoughts, my thoughts, His Will, my will; His Love, my love. This is holiness. He merited this grace for me; I have only to say, "I will."

My Motto: See Jesus *in* everyone. Be Jesus *to* everyone.

A Time of Decision

It is difficult to lead a Christian life today. The world has so much to offer, and, even though I find only emptiness, there are so many things waiting to fill the vacuum in my soul that God doesn't seem to have a chance. And then, one day, through the prayer of a friend, a sermon, or a book, my life begins to have meaning, and Jesus becomes real and alive in my soul. A whole new world opens up.

I begin to understand the love Jesus has for me, I notice all the little things He does, I see His hand and His love in many places, and suddenly I realize the things that held me in such bondage before have lost their meaning.

I seem alone in the midst of crowds. The things of the past no longer interest me and I cannot see the future. It is the time of decision. The seed has fallen to the ground and begun to germinate. The Lord and the world wait with expectation.

The best way to make any decision is to face it head-on and weigh all the pros and cons.

I Will Ponder . . .

Pro: If I choose the Lord, I will have joy and pain, but His strength will uphold me, and the reward is eternal.

Con: If I choose the world, there may be happiness here and there, but the pain will make me bitter, and the reward is passing.

Pro: If I spend some time each day in prayer, Scripture reading, and in an effort to see His love in everything, I will arrive at peace of soul and joy of heart.

Con: If I choose to fill my day with gossip, hours of television, and only fun and games, my day will be empty and my life more and more shallow.

Pro: The Love and joy that comes from Jesus in my soul will radiate to my neighbor and give him hope in times of despair.

Con: My best friends may think my new-found love is a threat to their lives and turn away from me.

Pro: In my business associations, I will see things and make decisions by Christian principles, giving fair wages, being honest and unprejudiced in dealing with employees—and thereby witness to my love for Jesus.

Con: I may possibly bring down upon myself the ridicule of my partners and associates, and be accounted as a fool and unrealistic for living by Christian principles.

Before I make a final decision, I must look at the Lord. Jesus chose me by accepting the opposition and ridicule of the majority as part of my salvation.

He didn't mind being considered a fool because He knew this was part of the price He had to pay so that I might enter the Kingdom.

He was content with influencing a few followers rather than huge multitudes because He knew that what *they* learned would be handed down to me intact.

It didn't bother Him that most of the people expected the Messiah to be more concerned with the present earthly needs of His people. He was determined I would realize by His examples that there was a better and higher life in the Kingdom.

He was happy to have a few friends accept Him as He was, rather than accept the applause of the crowds who cried aloud, "Hosanna to the Son of David" (Matt: 21:9).

He was brave enough to suffer the loss of all things, knowing that someday I would be asked to give up a few things.

My new life, then, as a Christian, is a matter of choices. Every day there are opportunities to choose the Lord, and I can do this without fuss and fanfare. My neighbor must not be made to feel that, now that I have found the Lord, he is not good enough for me.

The first Christians attracted pagans, not by quoting Scripture, but by having joy in the Lord in every circumstance, by love for everyone especially enemies, by breaking bread together, praying together, singing in their hearts, and having a beautiful assurance that Jesus is the Lord. They made Christianity so attractive that people flocked to join them.

The time for choosing has arrived. *I choose the Lord.*

The Life to Come

I know that life is a pilgrimage, a testing ground, and a time for growth. I must be aware of two realities — the visible that I can see and the invisible that I cannot see. My whole life must be geared toward a perfect harmony between these two realities.

If I look at only the visible and ignore the spiritual, I'm a fool; and if I see only the spiritual and ignore the visible, I'm unreal. Now that I have made a choice, I must maintain a balance between these two forces in my life.

The Lord told me to seek first the Kingdom of God and all other things would be added. He also promised that if I followed Him I would be rewarded a hundredfold in this life and life everlasting in the next.

I have seen what I must do and what rewards I will have in this life — but what of the next?

IN HEAVEN

God Himself will wipe away every tear from my eyes and sorrow will be no more.

There will be no disappointment, failure, or separation in the Kingdom.

Everyone without exception will love me and I will love them in return.

I will constantly learn new mysteries about God that will enlighten my soul and make it experience untold delights.

I will never again feel fear, distrust, or anger—only security, assurance, and perfect peace.

I will know the reason behind every pain and heartache during my earthly sojourn, and I will exclaim, "How great Thou art—to give so much for so little."

I will see the Father, Jesus, and the Holy Spirit Face to Face, and to sustain the joy of that experience God will give me the Light of Glory.

I will hear the same angelic voices heard by the Shepherds on that memorable night when Christ was born.

God will reward me because He is Good and wants me to be with Him and to enjoy all the things that ear has not heard or eye seen, and it will be all mine forever and ever.

Back to Earth

It often happens that after I have chosen to follow the Lord I suddenly feel a strange emptiness and a distaste for anything spiritual. I wonder what's wrong? Have I displeased the Lord? Has He withdrawn His Presence because of my unworthiness?

No—if I am sincerely trying to do His Will and love my neighbor, then I know this dryness is for my good. The Lord is purifying my soul of all selfishness so I may love Him for Himself alone. I will consider how I may grow strong in Faith, Hope, and Love, so that the reflection of Jesus in my soul will become brighter and glorify my Father.

Faith, Hope and Love

These three infused supernatural virtues, given to me at Baptism, are interwoven in my life like the petals of a flower. Faith tells me that what I believe in is *true*; Hope tells me the One I believe in is *faithful*; Love tells me the One I believe in is *mine*.

Faith is the virtue of the threshold; it makes me see in darkness now what I shall see by vision in eternity.

Hope is the virtue of the road; it assures me that I possess *now* what I shall possess in eternity.

Love is the virtue of the goal; it permits me to experience *now* what I shall delight in for all eternity.

Faith, Hope, and Love are three inseparable virtues, given to me by God so that in this "valley of tears" I may see Him in a "dark" manner, be assured that I possess Him, and be transformed by that possession. The test in this life is to believe what my senses do not perceive. It is by this complete confidence in His Word that I arrive at an abiding Love — a Love strong enough to make me give up my life rather than deny Him, and to love my neighbor in the same way He loves me.

Faith, in the Old Testament, was a belief in a God who made a Promise; Faith, in the New Testament, is a belief that the Promise has been fulfilled. Hope, in the Old Testament, was an expectation of One to come, but Hope, in the New Testament, is an assurance He is here. Love, in the Old Testament, was a measured response, and Love, in the New Testament, is a total surrender. In the Old Testament we learn that Faith gave Abraham a certainty that it was God who made him a Promise; Hope gave him assurance that the Promise would be fulfilled; Love gave him patience to await God's time.

Faith says He *can* do all things.
Hope says He *will* do all things.
Love says *whatever* He does is for my good.

Faith

What is Faith?

Faith is:

- an encounter in love between myself and God.
- a constant giving on God's part and a loving acceptance on mine.
- a prevention against being complacent, and a means of reaching for the invisible.
- believing what God has revealed just because He revealed it, and being content with the mystery I do not understand.
- believing that God is Love, and that somehow everything tends to good for those who love Him.
- opposed to fear, to hesitation, to worldly prudence and to anxiety for tomorrow.
- believing that God is at work in the depths of my being, despite darkness and obscurity.

- believing that His Power is at its best when I am weak.
- keeping the door of my soul open to Christ, the perfect image of the Father.
- an act of surrender by believing what I do not see.
- believing in His Personal Love for me and returning that love by allowing Him to change my life.
- never being disappointed with God's work in my soul or in my life.
- understanding that what I do to my neighbor I do to Him.
- seeing God in my neighbor regardless of his appearance.
- saying "Praise God" in adversity.
- seeing His Providence when He says "yes" and His Love when He says "no" to my requests.

My Progressive Growth in the Practice of Faith

I will thank God for the Gift of Faith and pray every day for an increase of this virtue which puts me in such loving contact with God. I will read Scripture and other books designed to increase my Faith and teach me how to see God around me and within me.

I will be careful not to bring the Wisdom of God down to my own level by refusing to believe those truths of Faith beyond my comprehension. When I begin to wonder "How do I know it's all true?" I will immediately turn to God and cry out, "I believe, Lord, help my unbelief" (Mark 9:24).

I will realize such doubts do not displease God but are permitted by Him to bring out a depth of Faith in me greater than the mustard seed.

I will look at the proof of His Word by the life of His Son, of Mary, and of all the holy men and women in the past and present. These examples will show me that only a loving God has the power to make poor human beings act like God.

Like these spiritual giants, I will continually seek to clear up any difficulty in Faith by consulting His Church and competent authority, and the advice of people close to God. I will go to the heart of Divine Mystery in order to grasp its meaning and apply it to my life. The Life of Christ will be a special source of light and strength. I will nourish my soul by the Sacraments so that I may abide in Him as He abides in me.

How Do I Share My Faith?

God's gift of Faith in me must bear fruit in my thoughts, actions, and dispositions. My neighbor must see the deep conviction of my Faith when he observes I prefer God to myself. I must share my Faith by encouraging the sick, poor, and unfortunate to bear patiently the sufferings and injustices of this life by bringing to mind the glory to come. By giving food to the hungry, comfort to the lonely, and compassion to the downtrodden, I will bear special witness to a deep Faith.

I will maintain a spirit of Joy in the midst of trials to show the Power of God in those who believe in Him. I will bear all things in the light of Faith — the Power of God in Creation, the Image of God in people, and the Providence of God in daily events. I will be faithful to the duties of my state in life as the best means of doing His Will and sharing My Faith. I will be of service to others, praying for their needs, and showing the love of Christ by loving them in the same way He loves me; this is the supreme test of faith.

Positive-Negative Aspects of Faith

Faith, in itself dark and obscure, gives me the power to "see" God.

Faith assures me that the aridity I experience at times is merely the darkness before the dawn.

Faith may not understand the mysteries of God but it penetrates their essence with a clarity it cannot explain.

Faith finds Joy in sacrifice and delights in giving.

Faith seeks more the God of Consolation than the consolations of God.

Faith grows stronger when there is little to hang on to.

It is when all seems lost that Faith shines as a brilliant star on the horizon, pointing to God's Providence and Mercy.

Faith directs the sinner to seek forgiveness.

Faith tells me that what I cannot see exists.

Faith tells me that what appears is passing, and what does not appear is everlasting.

Faith tells me that I shall find rest for my soul when I am meek and humble of heart.

Examples of Faith

To live by Faith in daily life is to:

- form a habit of seeing God in every person I greet every day.

- seeing His Will in all circumstances great and small, even in those things that are boring.
- seeing God in a change of plans, in uneasiness, and suffering.
- thanking God for every joyful, happy, and pleasant occasion in life.

The conversion of St. Augustine was the fruit of his mother's thirty years of prayer. Thomas More joked on his way to the scaffold and witnessed to his faith in the life to come. St. Therese of Lisieux and St. Jane Frances de Chantal suffered temptations against Faith for many years and used this trial to attain holiness. Matt Talbot, a hopeless alcoholic, overcame his weakness by putting his faith in God and not in himself. Pope John preserved serenity of soul in the midst of opposition because he realized God holds everything in the palm of His Hand. Mother Cabrini overcame bigotry with Faith in God and love for her neighbor.

SCRIPTURE

Blessed be God the Father of our Lord Jesus Christ who in His Mercy has given us a new birth as His sons, by raising Jesus Christ from the dead, so that we have a sure hope and the promise of an inheritance that can never be spoilt or soiled and never fade away, because it is being kept for you in the heavens. Through your Faith, God's Power will guard you until the salvation which has been prepared is revealed at the end of time. This is a cause of great joy for you, even though you may for a short time have to bear being plagued by all sorts of trials; so that, when Jesus Christ is revealed, your Faith will have been tested and proved like gold, only it is more precious than gold, which is corruptible even though it bears testing by fire-and then you will have praise and glory and honour. You did not see Him, yet you love Him; and still without seeing Him, you are already filled with a joy so glorious that it cannot be described, because you believe; and you are sure of the end to which your Faith looks forward, that is, the salvation of your souls. (1 Pet. 1:3-9)

But you, my dear friends, must use your most Holy Faith as your foundation and build on that, praying in the Holy Spirit; keep yourselves within the love of God and wait for the Mercy of our Lord Jesus Christ to give you eternal life. When there are some who have doubts, reassure them. (Jude 20-22)

Only Faith can guarantee the blessings that we hope for, or prove the existence of the realities that at present remain unseen. It was for Faith that our ancestors were commended. It is by Faith that we understand that the world was created by one word from God, so that no apparent cause can account for the things we can see. (Heb. 11:1-3)

Examine yourselves to make sure you are in the faith; test yourselves. Do you acknowledge that Jesus Christ is really in you? If not, you have failed the test. (2 Cor. 13:5)

Hope

What is Hope?

To most people, Hope is a sentiment that seeks some absent or distant good. On a natural level, it plays an important part in life; it is Hope that sustains a man in the performance of a difficult task: a farmer sowing his seed, a scientist seeking a new discovery, a politician running for office. This kind of hope is centered upon man himself and a trust in his fellowman. It is at this point that natural hope often wavers and ends in despair, because we soon realize that we are frail, changeable, and finite creatures, lacking in perfection and perseverance.

Supernatural Hope, however, sustains us in difficulties and disappointments for its emphasis is on the Faithfulness and Power of God, not on man. Although it, too, is a desire for a distant good (Heaven), it possesses the object of that desire (God) in this life. Supernatural Hope then gives me the assurance of a distant good *now*.

As humility is the foundation of Faith, Faith is the foundation of Hope. Faith tells me that God is Goodness, Beauty, Love, Wisdom, Providence, and Infinite Mercy; Hope gives me an assurance that this God, so Omnipotent, Majestic, and Good, is *mine*.

Hope:

- tells me that God not only wants me to be with Him in Heaven, but that He longs to live in intimate union with me *now*.

- tells me that my very misery attracts God's Infinite Mercy.

- tells me that God takes His delight in making me holy, especially when He has so little to work with.
- assures me that Infinite Mercy has forgiven my sins and gives me everything I need to live a holy life.
- gives me the certainty of His forgiveness.
- prevents me from being presumptuous or rash by thinking no effort on my part is needed to avoid sin.
- prevents me from being discouraged when I fall, for I hope with a *certainty* that God will do for me what my efforts alone can never do—make me holy.
- is to rejoice in my weakness, that the Power of God may be manifest.
- permits me to taste here below what I shall enjoy for all eternity.
- gives me strength to cooperate with God for my salvation and gives me assurance it will be accomplished.
- is "sure" because it is founded on God, on His Infinite Goodness and Sanctifying Power, not on my strength or weakness.
- is to throw myself upon God like a child in its mother's arms, with great trust regardless of how weak and powerless I feel.

- is to have full confidence in Christ because He lived and died for me.
- prevents me from withdrawing into myself after a fall.
- preserves my peace of soul in the midst of turmoil and tension.
- makes me rejoice when I am found worthy to suffer something for the Kingdom.

MY PROGRESSIVE GROWTH
IN THE PRACTICE OF HOPE

I know that God is Infinite Mercy and Infinite Justice, but if these two concepts are not harmonized perfectly by Hope, I run the risk of presuming on His Mercy by committing sin or despairing after sin by realizing His Justice.

Hope is an equalizer, a balancer, a harmonizer. It harmonizes these two attributes of Mercy and Justice in my life by giving me a childlike relationship with God as Father. This relationship bestows upon me courage to resist temptation out of love. I will never fall into a presumptuous attitude of offending such a Father just because He so easily forgives. However, I realize that sometimes I do offend God and it is then that Hope—bringing to mind my Father's Infinite

Mercy — keeps me from discouragement and despair. Hope gives me a deep realization that when I am truly sorry for my sins, and firmly resolved not to commit them again, He pardons me immediately.

God is magnificent when He pardons, and He never reproaches me for sins I have wept over and for which I have sought forgiveness. His pardon is so generous, so great and complete, that He not only annuls my debts but destroys even the memory of them as though they never existed.

Hope is truly the virtue of the middle road — the road between God's Justice and His Mercy. By walking in this sure path behind Christ — who is the Way and the Light — I have a joy that nothing will take away, a joy whose source is Christ, the Hope of the world. It is Hope in His Faithfulness that will sustain my joy in the midst of anxiety and turmoil. This is the kind of joy springing from Hope — that will be a witness to my neighbor that what I believe is true, and that what is true I possess.

Faith and Hope are so interwoven that at times Faith is a certainty that gives me assurance, and Hope is an assurance that gives me certainty.

I will make progress in this virtue by:

- being humble and not presuming on the Divine Goodness.

- not presuming on my own strength and rushing into occasions of sin.

- putting my confidence in Jesus and not in myself, realizing He can do all things.

- realizing that earthly joys are fleeting, but joy in the Lord is the beginning of eternal bliss.

- having an invincible trust that Jesus has gone on ahead to prepare a place for me.

- keeping in mind in times of adversity the living Presence of the Lord within me, saying, "Peace be to you. It is I. Fear not."

- a deep conviction that, although I am in difficulties on every side, I am never cornered; though I see no answer to my problems I never despair; though I am lonely I am never deserted; though I fail I am never a failure; though I am down I am never out; though all forsake me, God remains.

- manifesting an inner joy that shouts to my neighbor, "God dwells within."

- an assurance that His strength will never fail me.

HOW TO SHARE MY HOPE WITH MY NEIGHBOR

I will manifest Hope in my daily life by:

- an unhesitating confidence in the help of God.
- a desire for the "higher gifts" especially Love and Union with God.
- a Joy springing from within and not dependent upon material things.
- the desire to sow Hope where there is despair.
- a serenity that assures my neighbor all is well.
- an ability to raise up those who are discouraged, have fallen into sin, or have lost confidence in themselves.
- being positive and seeking out the good in everything and everyone.
- showing others it is possible to be *in* the world but not *of* the world.
- accepting praise or blame, sickness or health, success or failure, with equal grace.
- acknowledging my weakness and His Power in me.
- judging everything according to Christian standards rather than worldly standards.
- seeing myself as I really am and not being discouraged at the sight.

- keeping my eyes on God and depending on His strength to face the difficulties of my state in life.
- continuing to hope in His Providence to take care of me, my friends, loved ones, and world situations.
- realizing that the reward reserved for those who suffer innocently and unjustly will be beyond their wildest dreams.
- seeing good in everyone I meet, even the most depraved.
- having a positive outlook in every situation, especially the most impossible.
- knowing that it is easier to be a saint in the eyes of God than in the eyes of men.

POSITIVE-NEGATIVE ASPECTS OF HOPE

Hope:

- is the possession of a distant good.
- is purer the less there is to hang on to.
- makes everything possible that seems impossible.
- changes attitudes from darkness to light.
- gives joy to those who have been forgiven much.
- experiences a sense of loss at the death of a loved one but rejoices in their joy in the Kingdom.

- gives me courage to rise with confidence after every fall.
- gives me insight on how God brings good out of evil.
- makes me understand that acts of Hope in times of interior and exterior desolation are worth a thousand in times of joy.
- gives me assurance that an act of trust when I experience repugnance and abandonment is very pleasing to God.
- tells me I have only to "will" to trust and to have confidence in God — I need not "feel" trusting.

EXAMPLES

Abraham was assured by Hope that the Promise would be fulfilled even though year after year nothing happened.

The first Christians saw clearly that the sufferings of this life were not worth being compared to the glory to come.

St. Paul's Hope was invincible that he, too, would rise from the dead as Christ did.

Mary's Hope never wavered, even though she had to flee into Egypt with her Son.

So I will radiate a spirit of Hope by:

- realizing I am of more value than many sparrows.
- giving hope to all those I meet by being positive in my attitudes.
- saying with St. Paul that nothing shall separate me from Christ—neither tribulation, nor distress, nor persecution, nor famine, nor peril, nor sword. No—in all these things I will more than conquer Him who loves me.
- praying daily for strength and being courageous in difficult situations.
- understanding that my miseries attract the Divine Mercy—He delights in making something out of nothing.
- believing that God intervenes in every situation of my life.
- manifesting a quiet joy springing from an assurance that God loves *me*.

SCRIPTURE

For in Hope were we saved. But Hope that is seen is not Hope. For how can a man Hope for what he sees? But if we hope for what we do not see, we wait for it with patience. (Rom. 8:24-25)

May He enlighten the eye of your mind so that you can see what Hope His call holds for you, what rich glories He has promised the saints will inherit, and how infinitely great is the Power that He has exercised for us believers. (Eph. 1:18-19)

... sufferings bring patience, as we know, and patience brings perseverance, and perseverance brings Hope, and this Hope is not deceptive, because the love of God has been poured into our hearts by the Holy Spirit which has been given us." (Rom. 5:4-5)

When God wanted to make the heirs of the Promise thoroughly realize that His purpose was unalterable, He conveyed this by an oath; so that there would be two unalterable things in which it was impossible for God to be lying, and so that we, now we have found safety, should have a strong encouragement to take a firm grip on the Hope that is held out to us. Here we have an anchor for our soul, as sure as it is firm, and reaching right through beyond the veil, where Jesus has entered before us and on our behalf, to become a high priest of the order of Melchizedek, and forever. (Heb. 6:17-20)

Love

I have seen that Faith makes me adhere to God through knowledge, and Hope makes me adhere to God by an assurance that I possess Him now and I shall possess Him for all eternity — but there is something more to understand, and that something is *love*. Love is a tendency of the soul towards good, and so — Love means many things to many people. To some it is an impulse towards that which is agreeable to their senses and imagination: beauty, nature, people, and possessions. Others find love in whatever appeals to their reason and intellect — those dedicated to careers, science, etc.

But when the good I seek is only perceived by Faith, then that Love is supernatural — it is Christian Love. It is a Gift given to me at Baptism, and one I must grow in every moment of my life.

During the Last Supper discourse, Christ said, "I give you a new Commandment: love one another; just as I have loved you, you also must love one another" (John 13:34).

How Does Jesus Love Me?

He loved me before I was born. He loved me when I was a sinner.

He loves me with all my faults and imperfections.

As I am now, He is lovingly patient with all my infidelities.

He left all of Heaven to come down and teach me by word and example how to live.

He loves me as if no one else existed.

I am more valuable to Him than all of creation.

His Love for me is infinite and completely unselfish.

His Love is merciful—He rejoices when I seek forgiveness.

His Love is provident—He takes care of yesterday, today, and tomorrow.

His Love is personal—I am unique to Him.

His Love endures and does not diminish when I am unfaithful.

His Love seeks out my misery in order to bestow grace upon grace.

His Love gives me joy—just to know He really loves *me*.

His Love suffered all kinds of persecution to give me courage.

He loves me because He is good and His Love makes me better.

He loves me today, knowing I may be unfaithful tomorrow.

His Love is strong enough to run the risk of saying "no" when I ask for something that is not for my good.

His Love is patient when I prefer other loves to His.

His Love is kind—He does so many little things for me every day.

His Love is all-embracing—He is interested in the smallest details of my daily life—the very hairs of my head are all numbered.

His Love is humble—He stoops down and raises me up.

His Love made Him a servant when He prepared breakfast for His apostles at the Sea of Tiberias.

His Love desires to be loved in return.

His Love is not repulsed by my misery.

His Love gave every last drop of His Blood for me.

His Love is Powerful—it can transform me into Him.

His Love desires to bear fruit in my soul by my doing good to my neighbor.

His Love seeks to make me pleasing to the Father.

His Love calls me "friend."

His Love hovers over me, constantly on the watch, waiting for an expression of love from me.

His Love is attentive to my needs — He wants me to ask so that He may give.

His Love is more concerned with what I am than with who I am.

I will love my neighbor as Jesus loves me by:

- loving him as he is.
- being patient with his sins, faults, and imperfections, realizing I have a beam in my own eye.
- being of service and willing to be inconvenienced for the good of others.
- making others feel I think they are important to me.
- being unselfish and loving my neighbor first, and patiently waiting until he returns that love.
- making it easy for those who have offended me to ask forgiveness.
- assuring those who ask forgiveness that all is forgotten.
- providing for my neighbor's needs, temporal and spiritual, according to my means.
- listening and giving my neighbor the feeling I am deeply interested in everything about him.
- continuing to love after a neighbor has been unkind.

- being equally compassionate with those who are sick and those who imagine their sickness.

- loving my neighbor so much it proves to him there is a God.

- looking upon an enemy as a friend because he has given me the opportunity to forgive as my Father forgives.

- putting my neighbor at ease in an awkward situation.

- weeping with those who weep and laughing with those who laugh.

- manifesting a childlike candor and simplicity in dealing with others.

- protecting my neighbor's good name by not manifesting his faults to others.

- loving the sinner though I hate the sin.

- listening to opinions and suggestions with an open mind.

- not demanding that others be what I think they should be.

- helping those in need without making them feel that I'm condescending.

- being grateful for the least act of kindness shown me.

- realizing the offense I forgive is little in comparison with the offenses I have been forgiven.

- being meek and humble so that my neighbor will find rest for his soul.

- praying for all the needs of my neighbor and making his concerns my own.

- realizing nothing happens in my life that Jesus has not ordained or permitted for my good.

- showing my neighbor a joy independent of anything that happens.

- knowing everything in life is passing and that loving Jesus is a very important part of my life.

SCRIPTURE

Love is always patient and kind; it is never jealous; it is never boastful or conceited; it is never rude or self-ish; it does not take offense, and is not resentful. Love takes no pleasure in other people's sins but delights in the truth; it is always ready to excuse, to trust, to hope, and to endure whatever comes. (1 Cor. 13:4-7)

Beloved, let us love one another, for love is from God. And everyone who loves is born of God, and knows

God. He who does not love does not know God; for God is Love.

In this has the love of God been shown in our case, that God has sent His only begotten Son into the world that we may live through Him. In this is the love, not that we have loved God, but that He has first loved us, and sent His Son a propitiation for our sins.

Beloved, if God so loved us, we also ought to love one another. No one has ever seen God. If we love one another, God abides in us and His Love is perfected in us. In this we know that we abide in Him and He in us, because He has given us of His Spirit. And we have seen, and do testify, that the Father has sent His Son to be Savior of the world.

Whoever confesses that Jesus is the Son of God, God abides in him and he in God. And we have come to know, and have believed, the love that God has in our behalf. God is Love, and he who abides in love abides in God, and God in him. In this is Love perfected with us, that we may have confidence in the day of judgment; because as He is, even so are we also in this world.

There is no fear in Love; but perfect Love casts out fear, because fear brings punishment. And he who fears it is not perfected in Love. Let us therefore love, because God first loved us.

If anyone says, "I love God," and hates his brother, he is a liar. For how can he who does not love his brother, whom he sees, love God, whom he does not see. And this commandment we have from Him, that he who loves God should love his brother also. (1 John 4:7-21, NAB)

PRAYER

Lord, God and Father, You are Love; Your Son showed me Your Love and Your Spirit gave me Your Love. Grant me, Father, the grace I need to be Love, to show Love, and to give Love to my neighbor in the same way You have given Yourself to me. Amen.

HOLINESS IN ACTION

We read in the Gospels that Jesus emptied Himself when He came down to live in our midst. We realize the Eternal Word was made flesh and took upon Himself a humiliating existence — subject to the consequences of our sinner condition, but without sin. We know that part of His humiliation was to leave something and Someone great in order to live among lesser things and lesser beings. But was this all? If so, then none of us can empty his being of self, for we cannot go from something great to something lesser.

Simply then, our problem consists in how one grows in the Spirit of Jesus: resembles Him, thinks like Him, sees the present moment like Him, and empties his being of self. He assumed our nature so we could become sons of the Father.

Since we are to be holy in whatever state of life we are, wherever we are, whatever our talents, it is necessary for us to look deeper into the new commandment and see the answer to our dilemma.

The new commandment asks us to love each other in the *same way* Jesus loves us. To arrive at a solution as to the "how" of holiness, we will look only at one aspect of God's love for us. God loves us as we are at the moment and He loves us enough not to force our will to love Him in return or to force a change in us. He watches over us, moves us, broods over us, directs us, forgives us, gives us grace upon grace, extends His mercy when we repent and pricks our conscience when we refuse repentance, brings good out of the evil in our lives and gives us light to change.

His love constantly gives and adapts itself according to our will and disposition. He will not demand more than we can give, He will not force us to go further than we wish to go. He pours His love and grace upon us as we crawl, walk, run or fly towards Him.

Is this the secret of emptying ourselves? Is this how to love our neighbor? Is this how we change and then let that change change others? Is holiness something we pray for while waiting for the big event to happen, or is it a source of strength for ongoing growth?

People live, work, walk, play, shop, study, and eat with other people. There are few desert dwellers who live alone without depending in some way on people. Relationships, then, pose our biggest obstacle and our greatest aid to holiness. People are there, the command to love them given, but, unfortunately, our use of that command is meager. We sometimes think that loving means feeling affection, but God cannot command us to "feel." Love is a decision, but in what does that decision consist? Is it an act of the will that says "I love you" and then forgets the whole thing? Is it to forgive once in a while, hope the occasion never arises again and then become unloving when mercy is again in order? How do we empty ourselves so Jesus can radiate through us? Perhaps the one word that describes best what Jesus did and what we are to do is the word "accommodate." Every individual we meet is different than we are. Members of the same family differ one from the other. Friend differs from friend, husband from wife, sister from brother, nation from nation. All these differences make "feeling" love difficult and isolated to specific individuals according to our tastes and their personalities.

Jesus offered many helps and among them is the reality that what we do to the least, we do to Him. But even this is hard to do consistently, because we find it difficult to see Jesus in unpleasant situations, imperfect people and impossible circumstances. We are constantly waiting for others to be more Christ-like, thinking our response will be more peaceful. However, we cannot permit our responding to the call for holiness to depend upon the conversion, change or attitudes of others. What happens to us if *they* never change, never act like Jesus, never love us and are never converted?

What happens to our call to holiness when difficult situations occur and the people concerned are irritating, irritable and consistently vindictive? Does Jesus desire us to be as a reed shaken by the wind? Did He die and shed His Precious Blood so we would permit ourselves to be buffeted on every side by the passions, temperaments and other disagreeable traits of our neighbor?

Do we have legitimate excuses for our lack of virtue as we complain that obviously God did not call us to holiness since we do not live in a state of life devoid of "people" problems? Are we really saying that if it were not for "people" we could be holy? Yes, we are, and Jesus knew this when He gave us the new commandment.

Jesus dealt with everyone He met on the level of light, virtue and generosity at which their souls had arrived. He knew what the rich young man *could* do so He asked for all, but the man would not give all. It was, however, the rich young man who went away sad, not Jesus. Since the Source of Jesus' peace was the Father, He could ask, receive a "no," accept the person in his present state of soul and continue to love him.

Jesus knew what Judas would do when He called him, but this did not prevent Him from calling him. He dealt with Judas on the level where he was at the moment. Judas, at that moment was zealous, eager and looking forward to the Kingdom. Jesus accepted him where he was and as he was. He continued to love him by giving him light, warning him that we cannot serve two masters and enduring his bad dispositions.

Our reaction to people is the opposite of Jesus. We judge the motives we do not see, shortchange possibilities by the remembrance of past performances and then lose hope for any change that might occur in the future.

We also see how Jesus loved Peter. He called him, gently corrected his shortcomings, warned him of his coming denial, gave him a forgiving glance when he failed and forgave him completely when Peter made three acts of love. Never for a moment did Jesus even think of taking away the office He gave Peter as head of the Apostles. He saw his shortcomings, lived with them, made His plans around them, used them to make Peter grow and entrusted him with power and authority. *This* is loving.

We can be sure the Apostles were not always a comfort to Jesus. They did not understand His mission or His plan of redemption. His parables were beyond them, His desire for suffering a mystery, His revelations difficult to understand, His teachings too deep for their minds to penetrate. Sometimes He was so gentle they felt they could tell Him anything and then fear gripped their souls as they saw the Yahweh of the Old Testament, in the Person of Jesus, beating the money changers in the Temple. He made demands that seemed severe and made even more difficult when His life was an example of those demands. But these men followed Him, sacrificed for Him and that was loving Him.

We see then that Jesus grew in experimental knowledge and His Apostles made progress in grace and wisdom by mutual acceptance and by accommodating themselves to each other.

Jesus slowly brought their sense of values to higher levels by living His life according to those values. He spoke in parables to penetrate their level of light and intelligence. He forgave them often and then asked that they forgive seventy times seven. Knowing their repugnance for suffering, He would mention the coming Passion often and then soften the blow by the promise of His Resurrection. When they would ask Him questions that He had already answered, He would put forth sublime truths more simply without making them feel ignorant. He tried their patience by asking them to feed five thousand men with a few loaves and fishes and then multiplied that food to give them the joy of doing the impossible.

He had confidence in what was *inside* of them and patience to wait for it to blossom, but in the meantime, He met them where they were, knowing that the grace that came from rising would bring out those beautiful qualities hidden within.

His holiness brought out their darkness and that darkness disappeared in the Light. Once they learned to do to others as He had done to them, they too became lights in the darkness. They too were capable of bringing out of the most abject, beautiful qualities of soul. They became part of the Light "that enlightens all men" (John 1:9).

Perhaps we could call this ability "understanding adaptability." They themselves received Light from Jesus and since the Source of that Light was unending, that Light burst forth and touched others. St. Paul described this "adaptability" when he said, "everybody is to be self-effacing.... nobody is to think of his own interests first but everybody thinks of other people's interest instead. In your minds you must be the same as Christ Jesus; His state was divine, yet He did not cling to His equality with God, but emptied Himself to assume the condition of a slave" (Phil. 2:3-7).

The secret of emptying our being of self, of loving our neighbor as God loves us, of living the beatitudes is:

- To accept God on His terms.
- To accept ourselves as we are.
- To accept our neighbor as he is.

When we accept God on His terms, we do His Will—when we accept ourselves as we are, we realize our weaknesses and our total dependence upon His grace. This dependence makes us realize God's Will is superior to our own and this reality permits us to see our neighbor in a new light. We accept him as he is. When our neighbor is angry, then we are called by God to be gentle at that moment, for our neighbor is in need of *seeing* gentleness—we are self-effacing.

When our neighbor's personality possesses harsh qualities, we show our love by not voluntarily provoking those qualities in any way. Past experience shows us what upsets a person so in their presence we are careful not to do or say those things that cause anger. We are self-effacing. We are taking upon ourselves that person's weakness and lifting it up to God by acting like Jesus. This is what it means to "empty oneself and assume the condition of a slave." "Bear one another's burdens and fulfil the law of Christ" (Gal. 6:2). We are vigilant and watch for those things that please others—providing they are *not* sinful—avoid those things that annoy, adapt ourselves to their likes and dislikes, their talents and their weaknesses.

This puts us in a position of self-effacing love. We become living examples of the beatitudes. "You are light in the Lord; be like children of light," said St. Paul to the Ephesians, "for the effects of light are seen in complete goodness and right living" (Eph. 5:8-9).

When we adapt our conversation, our temperament, our knowledge, our virtue, our likes and dislikes to our neighbor's present state of soul, we are loving him as God loves him—we are a light in the darkness—we are Children of God. We truly follow St. Paul's advice: "Try, then, to imitate God, as children of His that He loves and follow Christ by loving as He loved you, giving Himself up in our place as a fragrant offering and a sacrifice to God" (Eph. 5:1-2).

This is dying to self, this is giving up our lives for our neighbor, this is holiness wherever we are, in whatever state we are. "A man can have no greater love than to lay down his life for his friends" (John 15:13). Few are called to actually lay down their lives for their neighbor, but we can all lay down our reactions, conquer our own weaknesses, put aside our very selves and accept our neighbor as he is at the present moment — and that is spiritual death.

Jesus did not always like the apostles' way of acting, but by adapting Himself to their temperament, praying for them to His Father, giving them a holy example of conduct, He loved them and that love changed them.

We find the apostles and the first Christians doing this very thing after Pentecost, for we read in the Acts: "The whole group of believers was united in heart and soul" (Acts 4:32). Unity of heart and soul is impossible unless everyone, or at least most, are "self-effacing, thinking of how to please others more than themselves." Jesus put it very graphically when He told the apostles, "You call me Lord and Master and rightly: so I am. If I, then, the Lord and Master have washed your feet, you should wash each other's feet" (John 13:13-15). Here He is speaking of each of us possessing a loving and humble spirit as we serve one another. That service is not only in things, but in bearing and forbearing, by careful anticipation of another's temperament and weaknesses, by self-effacing love.

To persevere in this bittersweet task of holy living we must maintain a deeply rooted vertical relationship with God, the foundation of which is humility and self-knowledge.

Spiritual Power cannot be contained within itself—it must go out to others.

Thus it is we are commanded to love God with all our strength, heart, mind and soul and our neighbor in the same way God loves us—it is the same love flowing between God and the soul, the soul and its neighbor.

It is difficult, but the burden of the cross is light compared to the cross of uncontrolled emotions, anger, insistence on one's own opinion, the frustration of trying to change others rather than being changed oneself, resentment, regrets and guilt. Accepting the present moment like Jesus did is certainly a lighter burden.

Grace is in whatever happens to you at the moment. How will you use it? For or against yourself?

"You who are holy brothers and have had the same heavenly call should turn your minds to Jesus" (Heb. 3:1).

In everything that happens, Jesus is sounding the call to holiness. *Let your lives ring out like a clear sounding bell: "Jesus is the Lord. Jesus loves you."*

THREE KEYS TO THE KINGDOM

OUTLINE 1
There Are Three Persons in One God
Father begets Son—Spirit proceeds from both
and
There Are Three Faculties in One Soul
Memory feeds Understanding—Will is fed by both

The Way It Is

As human beings, we are creatures of emotions, creatures of intellectual abilities, and creatures with the power to accomplish.

Some people spend their time and thoughts in feeling, hearing, seeing, and listening. Whatever cannot be felt or experienced they will not accept. We call these people emotional.

Some people spend their time reasoning and thinking out everything—and so—anything that cannot be fully understood, they will not accept. We call these people intellectuals.

Other people have only one goal in life, and that is to do as they please, when they please, and they impose their will on others. We call these people domineering.

When any of these people seek God in their own way, we find the emotional person seeking the consolations of God rather than God.

The proud intellectual seeks knowledge about God, but he never knows God, because he cannot accept the mysteries that he is unable to fully comprehend.

The domineering person seeks God and loves God as long as God does *his* Will. He cannot accept a "No" from God.

Most of us weave in and out of these three categories all our lives, and we never succeed in being changed into Jesus.

Christianity is a way of life, and it demands a change of heart and a change of mind. It entails a lifelong struggle to change our emotions, our way of thinking, and our way of acting.

We can relate with our emotions in regard to God or neighbor, and so as we look at our Memory to see how we can change it, we will quite easily grasp its role, its weaknesses, and its strength.

And so it is with the Will. We are all well aware of the strength of our Will and the Will of others. It has been the cause of success and failure, joy and sorrow, in our daily life. And so we shall understand the Will as we see its role and weaknesses and strength.

But this is not so true with the Intellect. *How* we understand, judge, discern, and form opinions, is a mystery — a mystery because the very faculty by which we understand does not comprehend *how* it understands.

We add Faith to our Understanding, and we give it light; to see things above itself. Faith is something that we have, but it too is something we cannot explain.

And when we say that we must be humble to have a deep Faith, we add an ingredient that is positively repugnant, to something that is already difficult to grasp.

And so, when we get to the faculty of our soul that we call Understanding, we will have to plow a little deeper; so the seeds that will be sown can reap a rich harvest of a new way of thinking.

Our Christianity changes and transforms us from sadness to joy, from darkness to light, and from slavery to freedom. We must seek the way to this "spiritual revolution" that we may be set free from ourselves and live in Him and by Him. We must be a witness to a sad world, of Heaven on earth, of peace amidst turmoil, and joy amidst pain.

So we shall look at our Memory — not to dig in, but to root out.

We shall look at our Understanding — not to comprehend but to utilize.

We shall look at our Will — not to lose it, but to redirect it.

OUTLINE 2
Made in His Image

Our Memory resembles the Father — as the Father knows Himself, we know ourselves through our Memory.

Our Understanding resembles the Son — as the Son is the perfect Image of the Father, so our Understanding is the exterior image of what we remember.

Our Will resembles the Spirit — as the Holy Spirit is the Love and Power that proceeds from the Father and the Son, so our Will is motivated by love and accomplishes what the Memory and Understanding give it to desire.

First Key: Memory & Hope

The Apostles often found the words of Jesus difficult to understand and they told Him so. But during the Last Supper, when He spoke of His Father and the Father's personal love for them, they finally began to understand.

Jesus looked at them and said, "Do you believe at last? Listen — the time will come — in fact, it has already come — when you will be scattered, each going his own way and leaving Me alone. And yet, I am not alone, because the Father is with Me. I have told you all this so that you may find peace in Me. In the world you will have trouble, but be brave; I have conquered the world" (John 16:31-33).

His first words after His Resurrection were "Peace be with you! Why are you so agitated, and why are these doubts rising in your hearts?" (Luke 24:37).

Why was Jesus disappointed in His Disciples' lack of faith? It would seem, at least on the surface, that the Apostles had every right to be sad and agitated.

Their Master was taken away from them, tortured, and crucified. Their Memories of His kindness and gentleness only made their hearts more agitated and bitter.

Their Imaginations projected fear into the future, and a feeling of hopelessness took possession of their souls.

They remembered how they thought He would deliver them from tyranny, and now it was all over.

What happened to these men that would cause Jesus to ask the reason for their sadness? What did He expect them to do? Why did He wonder at their lack of peace?

All during His public life He asked them to believe in Him, to trust Him, and to abide in Him. Apparently, they did none of these things when the test came, else He would not have questioned their agitation.

It would seem from reading the Scriptures that the Apostles were men of great ambition and imagination.

They realized by His signs that Jesus was Lord, but their concept of the Messiah was material and self-centered.

They often argued as to which one was the greatest, and James and John decided to be on the right and left of Jesus in the Kingdom.

They greatly rejoiced in the powers Jesus gave them, and imagined themselves on twelve thrones judging the twelve tribes of Israel.

For three years they listened to His Words, but they repeatedly admitted they did not understand His parables.

They rejected the thought of His future suffering though He revealed it to them beforehand. At one time Peter tried to dissuade Him from going to Jerusalem, and Jesus called him Satan.

It is obvious from these incidents that although they had the grace to believe in His Sonship they did not as yet live a life of Faith.

They began to live on an emotional level—a level in which their daily lives were guided by their Memories and Imaginations. They no longer *used* these faculties; they *lived* in them.

When we live our daily lives *in* these faculties, then we live in ourselves and not in God.

We are *living in* these faculties

- when we harbor resentments and refuse to forgive and forget,
- when we worry about tomorrow to the extent that it paralyzes us in the present moment,
- when we seek only our own pleasure in everything, unconcerned with the needs of others,
- when normal discouragement over failures turns into depressing sadness,
- when the remembrance of past sins turns into guilt complexes,
- when a desire to succeed turns into greed and double-dealing,
- when a normal desire to be loved turns into suspicion —and lust,
- when a need to relax turns into over-indulgence in food, drink, and recreation,
- when the need to be needed turns into jealousy and possessiveness.

Yes, when these wonderful faculties become the master in the temple of our souls, then we run the danger of becoming slaves in our own household—prisoners, bound hand and foot, swayed to and fro "like a reed shaken by the wind" (Matt. 11:7).

Jesus asked the crowds one day exactly what they expected to find in John the Baptist—"a reed shaken by the wind?" No, John was a Prophet whose Will was united to God's Will and who lived by his Understanding and not by his ever-changing emotions. He was a man who was master of his own house and he used his emotions at the right time and in the right place. The Spirit of the Lord could use him to lash out at Herod and to tell the people to repent. He did this with all the emotion of one led by God, and used his lower faculties for God's honor and glory.

We are human and we understand emotions, for they convey ideas and goals in a way that many words fail to do. This is why they were given us but we must use them for God's honor and glory.

We must put these faculties to work for us in order to live a fuller life, but we must never reach the point where we are not in control.

The real danger comes when we use these faculties to love with, for we run the risk of loving with a selfish love. We will love only those who love us. Our enemies or those with whom we have little in common, we will not love at all.

We will love only those who render us a service; and those who, for one reason or another, are not able to comply with our demands, we will ignore or treat coldly.

The things that excite our Imagination and passions will be sought after, and we will run the risk of weakening our Wills and acting in an unreasonable manner.

Living in these faculties, instead of using them, means being tossed to and fro on a perpetual seesaw. One day we are up on the heights of joy, and the next day down to the depths of despair.

As long as we permit our life to be regulated by these faculties we will never possess the Peace He left to us. The Commandment to love our neighbor in the same way God loves us will become almost impossible to obey.

A Christian does not pretend or talk himself out of his problems or pains. He faces them head on, and feels their impact, but he rises above them to the level of faith and trust. He is a marvel to behold as he accepts life and all its trials with Peace and Resignation.

We are human and we have feelings—feelings we cannot deny or negate. Each one of us is different but we will spend our entire lives eating and drinking, laughing and crying, happy and sad, succeeding and failing. But no matter what we do, it must be done for the honor and glory of God and the good of our neighbor.

We have Jesus as our model in using these faculties. We see Him during His public life receiving ingratitude and insults over and over again. Yet, He was always in possession of His soul. He held His Peace and never let His Memory of past ingratitude interfere with His kindness in the present moment.

Though He knew exactly what was in store for Him, He did not permit His Imagination to bring fear and repugnance to His soul.

He could look out into the crowd, know the thoughts of each person and still speak of love and compassion to the few who understood.

He would use these faculties for the purpose for which they were given; and all during His Agony and Death He never allowed Himself to be swayed by the jealousy and hatred of His enemies.

He used His emotions for the Father's honor and glory and our edification.

It was the emotion of Compassion that made Him raise the widow's son to life.

It was Sorrow that made Him weep at the news of Lazarus' death. He wept over Lazarus in spite of the fact that in a few moments He intended to exert His power and raise him from the dead.

He used the emotion of Anger to throw the moneychangers out of the Temple and to pronounce seven woes on the Pharisees.

Yes, He was human and He used human emotions as servants to express love, concern, sympathy; He manifested anger over the injustices that His creatures heaped upon each other. But He never *lived* in these faculties.

How different He was from His Apostles. They lived with Him long enough to understand, but their Memory and Imagination had not yet become servants, and they were disturbed very often over petty things — like which one of them was the greatest.

It may be well to look at some of these first Disciples' and learn from their mistakes.

In the Garden of Olives Jesus asked Peter to pray lest he be tested and fail. But Scripture tells us that Peter was so grieved over the prospect of the Master's suffering and death that he fell asleep.

It was perfectly normal for Peter to feel concerned and troubled over what was to come. It is always difficult to see those we love suffer — in fact, we call this concern, Compassion. But Peter did not use this emotion to spur himself on to prayer and meditation. He permitted it to take possession of him and make him sad to the point where he became discouraged.

He began to feel helpless and hopeless and went to sleep in an effort to blot the sorrow from his memory. He failed when the test came because his faith was not strengthened by prayer and compassion.

Jesus, on the other hand, had also felt fear of the suffering to come, but He did not live in that fear even for a moment. Though the fear was strong enough to make Him sweat blood and ask that the chalice be taken away, He rose above it and lived in His Understanding by presenting to Himself the necessity of this hour for the Redemption of mankind and the acquiescence of His Will to the Father's Will.

Many times during His life He told us not to worry about tomorrow, because to worry is to project a feeling of hopelessness in the future. This is a misuse of our Memory and Imagination (Matt. 6:33-34).

He realizes we must plan for the future, but we can plan without worry. God has given each one of us talents and He expects us to render an account of them. The use of these talents often entails the planning of future projects to render a service to mankind, but here again He does not want us to worry.

We use the talents we possess to the best of our ability and leave the results to God. We are at peace in the knowledge that He is pleased with our efforts and that His Providence will take care of the fruit of those efforts.

At another time Jesus said, "If a man looks at a woman lustfully, he has already committed adultery with her, in his heart" (Matt. 5:28). This is a perfect example of misusing our Memory and Imagination.

Our Imagination is greatly influenced by our senses. Our eyes see, and a picture is imprinted upon our Memory. Our nose smells, and our mouth waters with the aroma. Our ears hear, and we are calmed or frightened by the sound. Our tongue tastes, and we rejoice in the variety of foods that delight our appetite. Our sense of touch can make us feel warm with the embrace of a loved one or shiver from cold as we face the wind.

All these senses affect our Memory and Imagination and together they make life enjoyable and livable. They are good, and designed by God to enhance daily living with beauty, joy, and laughter. They also warn us of danger when we touch the flame of a match and feel pain. They remind us to eat by a pain in our stomach, and thrill our hearts when we see the beauty of a sunset.

These faculties render us a service by a feeling of fear sometimes—a kind of intuition that warns us of danger or pain. The memory of slipping on an icy sidewalk makes us careful as our Imagination relives the incident so vividly that we can feel the pain of the fall.

All these wonderful services are rendered by these faculties, but if we misuse them, as in the case of the man looking upon a woman with lust, then we turn these faculties against God—the Supreme Giver, and against ourselves. We use them for evil purposes and totally forget their original purpose in our lives.

It is true that we cannot always help or prevent the rapid pictures and thoughts that enter our minds, but we can prevent the entertaining of those thoughts, and the occasions that promote them. And this is what Jesus warned us of when He said the man "looked" at the woman. It was a deliberate act to excite his Memory and Imagination for evil purposes.

We must remember that to give in is to live in, and so the man had already committed adultery with her in his heart.

The statement "How will I know unless I try," has been the cause of great evil in our lives. A young girl wants to try dope to feel its effects, and it unbalances these faculties to the extent that it is nearly impossible to reestablish balance.

And so it is with every other evil. If all we think of is satisfying our sense of taste, we can become gluttons in food or drink. If we desire to experience everything there is in life to experience, then we face the danger of running these beautiful faculties into the ground and living on an animal level. Our Will becomes so weak that we live almost by instinct instead of as intelligent human beings.

We can also live in these faculties to the extent that the fire of hate is enkindled at the least provocation. We can feed this fire with the straw of past offenses until the wind of our Imagination takes over and we are destroyed by the rage of hate and bitterness.

Even our prayer life and good deeds can be lived in this faculty — the Imagination — and instead of using our Memory to recall and realize some incident in the Lord's life that we may imitate Him, we concoct methods of showing off our good deeds and spiritual life so as to attract the attention of others.

Jesus warned us to be careful not to parade our good deeds before men to attract their notice. He wants us to witness to His Power in our lives by good example, but the motive for them must be His honor and glory, not just a way of attracting attention to ourselves.

He said that our left hand must not know what our right hand is doing. In other words, we must be careful that our Memory does not mentally rehearse our good works in a way that our Imagination pats us on the back with a wonderful, wonderful feeling that we are so very good (Matt. 6:1-4).

Our Memory in this case should bring to mind the Goodness of God in our regard, and our Imagination be used only to invent new ways of helping our neighbor in his trials and needs. They are not to be used to compliment ourselves and show us off before men.

This is also true in our spiritual lives. Jesus said that we are not to imitate the "hypocrites who pray standing in the Temple and on street corners for people to see them" (Matt. 6:5). To invent ways to pray so that others can see us and think of us as holy individuals, takes a great deal of Imagination; and the Memory of past compliments will prod us on to even greater heights of folly.

Our Memory and Imagination can be used in a most marvelous way in our prayer life, but the emphasis must be on God, not ourselves. Since all things are present to God, we can use our Memory to recall an incident in the life of Jesus, and then our Imagination can put into that scene all the visual props necessary to "see" it in our minds.

We can recall Jesus sitting on a large rock in the cool of the night, resting from a tension-filled day. Our Imagination can picture ourselves going over to Him, sitting beside Him, and taking His hand in ours to give Him comfort.

After our Memory has rendered us that service, our Understanding and Will can take over, that is, our Faith and Love. Then we can speak to Him as a friend speaks to a friend.

Our Understanding and Will are areas known only to God and ourselves. He alone knows the light we possess and the direction of our Will, and so Jesus says, "But when you pray, go to your private room and, when you have shut your door, pray to your Father, who is in that secret place, and your Father who sees all that is done in secret will reward you" (Matt. 6:6).

The "private room" is our Will and Understanding, and, we must shut the door of our Memory and Imagination lest they disturb us with the past or future and clamor for attention as we go into that "secret" chamber with the Bridegroom of our souls.

We must both live and pray in the areas of Understanding (where Faith resides), and our Wills (in which Love resides).

It is in our Faith and Love that we dwell with God and God dwells with us. We cannot permit our Memories to disturb our communion with God by recalling past failures or allow our Imagination to embellish those failures to make us feel unworthy to possess such a loving friendship with God.

We can misuse these faculties so that a pall of sadness falls upon us and blots out all joy as well as the power to Reason and to Will.

We have an example of this in the disciples going to Emmaus (Luke 24:13-35). They saw their Master tortured, crucified, and die an ignominious death, all of which was not in their plans for setting Israel free.

In their disappointed frame of mind they decided to go away from Jerusalem, the scene of their frustrations and lost hopes. Though all seemed lost to them, they did the one thing that saved them—they continued to speak of the Master. Perhaps we could call this a "disgruntled prayer."

Jesus drew near, and Scripture says, "something prevented them from recognizing Him" (Luke 24:16). There were two reasons for this lack of recognition: first, the glorified body was in a new condition—its outward appearance changed; secondly, their Memory and Imagination blinded their intellect and weakened their Faith. Their minds were clouded with thoughts of disappointed hopes.

This is a perfect example of spiritual blindness. It is possible to be so weighed down in an attitude of hopelessness that we cannot see the answer to our problems—even when that answer stands before us.

We can become totally absorbed in these two faculties until our Intellect is not able to reason clearly. The disciples were living in the sorrowful past, and their Imaginations projected a hopeless future.

When Jesus drew near, they were not ready to see Him. This is a level that many people never rise above. They constantly live in an unhappy past or a miserable future.

Their only hope lies in the fact that many of them continue to pray, just as the disciples continued to speak of Jesus despite their sadness.

Before they could see Him, Jesus had to raise them to a Faith level; He had to release them from themselves so that they would not only speak of Him but begin to live in Him. Their whole minds were to be absorbed in Him. It was not enough to speak of Him in disappointed tones.

This is how many of us pray. We do not live in our thoughts of Jesus; we merely speak to Him in disgruntled tones of disappointment because our requests are not granted in the way we had imagined.

Jesus demands Faith, and all during His life He looked for the kind of Faith that believed because it trusted, and trusted because it loved.

As Jesus drew near and asked them what they were speaking about, they were a little short-tempered and said, rather impatiently, "You must be the only person staying in Jerusalem who does not know the things that have been happening these last few days" (Luke 24:18).

When we live in our Memories we just cannot understand why everyone else cannot share our own sentiments. Our busy world of the past is so filled with ourselves, and our reasons for being sad are so clear to us, that we cannot understand why everyone doesn't feel exactly as we do. If that Memory is filled with hate for a particular person, we cannot fathom how anyone could love that person. If it is filled with sadness, we cannot imagine anyone joyful. If it is filled with resentment, we cannot imagine anyone merciful. If it is filled with bitterness, we cannot imagine anyone kind.

Like the disciples going to Emmaus, we are either intolerant or impatient with anyone who is not living in the same world we live in.

Jesus asked them what happened that caused them to be so downcast. But because they were living in the past, their answer was in the past tense.

"We *had* hoped," they told Him, "that He would be the one to set Israel free" (Luke 24:21).

They *had* hoped. In other words, they hoped no longer. His death proved to them that He was not the one they were waiting for.

Once these disciples lost hope, their Understanding became completely muddled, as their next statement proves. "And this is not all," they continued, "two whole days have gone by since it all happened and some women from our group have astounded us: they went to the tomb in the early morning, and when they did not find the body, they came back to tell us they had seen a vision of Angels, who declared He was alive. Some of our friends went to the tomb and found everything exactly as the women had reported, but of Him they saw nothing" (Luke 24:21-24).

These men had definite plans as to what the Master was to do—even His rising from the dead was imagined by them. They heard Him say several times that He would rise on the third day, and they, no doubt, imagined that Angels would blow trumpets, all the people would run to the tomb, and the Master would rise in triumph and begin to rule their nation. Yes, nothing would stop them. They would rule the world.

They had heard the Master speak of higher things, but, as He spoke they used His words only to plunge deeper' within themselves. They had definite plans and ideas and they made His words fit those plans.

They never seemed to be able to rise above a narrow level of Understanding. When the women told them the tomb was empty they became more discouraged and decided to get away from all this nonsense.

They walked away from a truth that came from God, to look for a truth that would fit their own ideas. But their power to understand was so weakened by their uncontrolled emotions that they could not see the real truth.

It is not only the cares of this world that choke the Word in our hearts, it is the invisible daydreams, neatly planned and lovingly clung to, that create a cloud of unreality around us. It can become a way of life—a life of unrealized ambitions or uncontrolled hatreds.

We may pride ourselves that all we feel is justified, in the same way as these disciples did. We can find good reasons for every ill-tempered moment of our lives. But, somehow, down deep, our inner soul cries out for release from the slavery of its passions—it seeks to rise above itself and live in the peace of His Spirit, and in the possession of His Truth.

The disciples did not understand that there was only one way to accept the Crucifixion and the Agony of the past few days, and that was to rise above it and not fall beneath it or run away from it.

They had already fallen under the weight of suffering, and now they were trying to escape from everything and everyone who reminded them of those trying days.

One thing they did not understand, and that was that their real problems were within. They were the cause of their unrestrained emotions. Even when the women assured them of the empty tomb, they simply refused to be comforted.

They nurtured their wounds by rehearsing all the scenes that were responsible for their sadness and no comforting words could enter within them.

As their problem was emotional, nothing emotional could help them. They felt the women were hysterical and not worthy of credence.

They had lived for three days in their memories and now it was time to rise above this level to the level of faith.

Jesus said to them, "Foolish men! So slow to believe the full message of the Prophets. Was it not ordained that the Christ should suffer and so enter into His glory?" (Luke 24:25-26).

Yes, they understood part of the message but not the full message. As they listened to the Master, their emotions had accepted only those things that appealed to them—the honor, the glory, and the prestige. Their Understanding was never allowed to reason out the necessity of the Christ's suffering and death. This was deeper than their reason could fathom—it was on the level of faith, and to this level they had not as yet ascended.

Then Jesus began to explain the Scriptures to them. He started with Moses and went throughout the Scriptures, explaining those passages that referred to Him.

Slowly, as He explained, their minds were turned away from themselves and became centered on Him. They began to reason with their intellects instead of their emotions. They were no longer merely talking *about* Him—they were living *within* Him. As He spoke, they began to see the purpose of His suffering. They realized that it was foreseen as something necessary in order for the Christ to enter into His Glory and redeem mankind.

Suddenly, everything made sense, and after they recognized Him in the breaking of bread, they remembered that their hearts burned within them as He spoke.

Yes, they still had emotions as their Memory recalled every passage He brought to mind, but now they were free of themselves and set on God. Their Memories were being used to serve their reasoning powers to arrive at a logical conclusion—a conclusion that their Wills could accept.

Are we saying the disciples should not have felt grieved over their Master's death? No, it was human and necessary that they express their sorrow over the injustice and cruelty of His Death.

But this was not the real cause of their sorrow. They were grieved more over their disappointed hopes than the injustice of His suffering. They felt a sense of loss over His Death, but even this was for selfish reasons. To them, His Death meant more tyranny from the Romans and little chance of liberation.

Their Wills had chosen to be guided by their Memory and Imagination, and as a result their souls were cast into sadness and grief.

We see this identical thing in the case of Mary Magdalene. The Lord had forgiven her many sins and freed her of seven devils. She witnessed His suffering and grieved over His Death.

She, too, heard Him say He would rise on the third day, but this woman, who had lived her entire life on an emotional level, saw nothing in all that happened but darkness and desperation.

Even the sight of Angels could not dispel the darkness. She was completely absorbed in her loss, and her Will had chosen to live in the emptiness of a loved one gone forever.

We can look at Elias in the First Book of Kings and find one of many who succumbed to the danger of discouragement.

He had succeeded in showing the people the true God as fire came from Heaven to consume the evening sacrifice. But when Jezebel sent Elias the message that he would be as dead as the four hundred and fifty Prophets he had killed, he ran away. He fled into the wilderness and sat under a furze shrub and asked God to take away his life.

In accomplishing God's Will, he succeeded only in making himself a hunted man. His Imagination drew pictures of a hopeless situation, and the man who performed miracles gave in to a depth of sadness nigh unto death.

As he slept under the tree, an Angel of the Lord appeared to him and gave him a hot scone to eat and water to drink. But, like Mary Magdalene, the sight of an Angel meant nothing. He was satisfied in his misery. His sadness was a kind of anesthetic that numbed his faculty to reason, and blotted out the next arduous course to take.

It was an easy road, sitting under a tree feeling helpless, with a perfect excuse not to do anything else to further God's Kingdom.

All three of these accounts show how we can and often do live in our Memory and Imagination. We love to hash over bitter experiences in order to justify our own weaknesses. We project the future as a continuation of our unhappy past and begin to live in a world of unreality.

We call it being realistic because we know what the past has been and knowing ourselves we can mentally predict the future. But it is all very unreal because even a bitter past can be used to our advantage, and our faith assures us that the One who brought us into the world will take care of every detail of our lives.

It seems to our finite minds, however, that God does not really know every circumstance and incident that makes us what we are. We want so much to be justified in our anger, hatred, resentment, ambition, and greed.

All these disturbing thoughts press in upon our Memory and Imagination, and we begin to actually live in these faculties. Everything that happens to us during the day is somehow related to some past incident, and tension mounts upon tension until our whole life is torn up by Memories and Imagined frustrations.

It is as if a million tiny webs cover our being, blotting out the light of grace and the air of peace.

We are tied down and hampered by our own faculties, and because they are so close to us we cannot emerge from the darkness.

What is the solution to this problem? Are we to become stoical and cold? Are we to pretend we have no problems or feelings? Are we to blot all feeling from our souls by some feat of Will Power?

The answer to all these questions is *no!* At the risk of being repetitious, it must be said again and again that our Memory and Imagination are *gifts* from God and must be used as a key to unlock a depth of Faith that is hidden in our Understanding.

When we are offended we feel hurt—so hurt sometimes that tears fill our eyes to express our emotions.

When we are hurt, we do not have a problem as much as an occasion to be like the Father, who lets His sun rise on the good and the bad. But many times what is permitted by God for our sanctification becomes a problem when we do not release it the moment it happens. If anything disturbing is not blocked out by the light of Faith, it drains all hope from our souls. It becomes a problem, and a problem that may be with us the rest of our lives.

At Baptism we were given the Theological Virtue of Hope, to elevate our Memory to a higher level. We are not only to store the experiences and the accumulated knowledge of everyday life, but we can now store the living words of

God's Son, His Revelations, and His life and example, in order to overcome our disturbing Memories and overworked Imagination.

The recalling and retention of these living Words permits our Memory to rise above the things of this world and to live in the Word of God.

Through Prayer and Scripture and the Sacraments, our Memory begins to store good things and to put aside the rancor that keeps it in a constant turmoil.

It begins to live on a supernatural level—seeing all things in the light of Hope. When it recalls an offense, it should substitute the words of Jesus and remember how He forgave and how He used every opportunity that came His way for the Honor and Glory of the Father.

When the Memory recalls a failure, it should immediately substitute the life of Jesus. The seeming failure of His Mission turned out to be the greatest success the world has ever known.

When the Memory recalls a past sin that looms ahead like a giant monster to devour us, it must substitute many passages of Scripture and Parables that show the Mercy of God towards His people.

When our Imagination begins to torture us with various pictures of glory or despair, our Memory must recall the humility of Jesus—to quiet our ambitions, and must recall the Mercy of God—to raise us up from despair.

When our Imagination projects a future that is dark and miserable, our Memory should recall God's Providence—to assure us of His concern and protection.

When our Imagination telescopes all our problems until they look unsurmountable, our Memory must recall the words of Jesus when He said that if we had the faith of a mustard seed we could move mountains.

We must substitute a good thought for a disturbing thought. The substitution process is a *positive* way of overcoming our faults and changing our lives.

If the substitution is on the natural level, it may bring a change of thought but not a change of *life* that will effect our union with God.

If someone offends us by some cutting remark, we can immediately substitute a mental picture of a lotus flower in a calm lake. If our Imagination is strong enough, it may change our pattern of thought and calm our anger. And if we make a habit of thinking beautiful thoughts in the midst' of chaos, it may become a habit that gives us a natural serenity. This kind of substitution may lead to control, but will not lead us above ourselves to a supernatural level.

The change we pattern for ourselves must be super natural, not natural. A change on the natural level may make us better human beings, but will *never* make us radiate the image of Jesus.

One day Jesus said, "I am the Way, the Truth, and the Life. No one can come to the Father except through Me" (John 14:6).

He is the Way by which our Memory and Imagination must be held in control. He is the Truth that our Understanding clings to in order to rise above its limited capacity to see the Mysteries of God. He is the Life, that is, Love, by which our Wills are made strong enough to overcome the greatest obstacles, as we journey Home.

Yes, we must substitute the Words and Life of Jesus to arrive at the truth of every situation. Our entire life is an exercise by which our souls are molded and changed, for better or worse, by the way we use every situation, disappointment, joy, or sorrow.

We must strive to live a holy life — the life of a son of God, not only a good life as a mere creature of God.

Only God can give us supernatural life. Only Jesus is the Way, the Light, the door of the sheepfold, and the Resurrection. Only through Him can we rise from a life of imperfection to a life of holiness.

This is why, at Baptism, He has given each faculty of our soul an infused Virtue — to raise it above its natural level that it may live in Him.

- To raise our *Memory and Imagination* to a higher level He has given us the Virtue of Hope. Hope assures us of His Love and Mercy to quiet the memories of a sinful past, and reminds us of His tender Justice to prevent us from becoming presumptuous.

- To raise our *Understanding* to a higher level, He has given us Faith. It is Faith that raises a finite mind with a limited reasoning power, to the heights of God — gazing upon hidden Mysteries as a child revels in the perfections of its father.

- To raise our *Will* to a higher level He has given us Love. It is Love that spurs our Wills on to heroic deeds, to sacrifice, and to joy in the midst of suffering and persecution. Jesus' Death and Resurrection merited grace for each one of us. Grace — a Divine Participation in

His Nature, raises our souls from a natural level to a supernatural level.

As our natural life is a gift from God, so this new birth in Christ is a gift from God. It is something that must grow each day by our taking advantage of every opportunity to become more like Jesus.

The spiritual faculties of a Christian must be elevated to a higher plane. Though he fail often, the Christian ever seeks to unite his will to God's Will, and he knows how to take advantage even of his failures.

The Infused Virtues are there in seed form, ready for us to water by our effort, in order that He may bear fruit in us.

We need not fear when our emotions seem to take control. As long as we continue to make an effort to control them, Jesus Himself will come to us and bless our efforts with success.

Life is not a Utopia; it is a proving ground; and a Christian must be able to use every kind of situation to his advantage.

Jesus said, "This people honors me only with lip-service, while their hearts are far from me" (Mark 7:6).

To speak of our hearts is to speak of our emotions, and we must give the faculties of our Memory and Imagination to the

Father, that the faculty, made to His Image and Likeness, may beget Jesus in our souls.

To accomplish this task and cooperate with the Spirit in renewing these faculties, we must look upon everything through the eyes of Hope.

It is a lack of Hope that makes our Memory retain resentments and our Imagination project fear into the future.

Our Memory will always bring back people and circumstances from our past that may disturb us, but it is only when we deliberately entertain these thoughts and encourage them that they take possession of us and we fall under their power.

It doesn't matter what kind of disturbing memory haunts us, Hope assures us that God brings good out of evil for all those who love Him.

It is because we make so many exceptions to this rule that we never seem to move forward in holiness.

We know God is with us in one particular situation, but we doubt His Providence in another. There are times in our life when our Memory completely blanks out God's past intervention, or care of us, and we are left alone on the sea of life.

Hope is that virtue that makes our Memory recall God's plan in our moment to moment existence. It gives us the ability to substitute other memories more positive and assuring.

The Beatitudes are counsels of Hope that are positive aids in every negative situation. It might be well to look at the Beatitudes to see how they are in truth an example of Memory control and the fruit of Hope.

Blessed are the poor in spirit; theirs is the Kingdom of Heaven. To be poor in spirit is to be detached from the things of this world, but most of all, detached from ourselves.

How much control of our Memory and Imagination is necessary to be detached! Our Memory can recall past successes, and our Imagination live in the ventures to come—all of which will be as successful as the past. These two faculties can make us ambitious for honors, glory, and riches, not for *His* sake, but solely for our own sake.

We can spend hours reveling in our self-esteem, and no-one can enter into that inner sanctum of self—not even God. Yes, we can become very much attached to our talents, successes, position, and petty ambitions—so much so that we live in a dream-world, where the entire population is me, myself, and I.

But we must accept the pain of detachment from earthly things, as the Virtue of Hope reminds us of the eternal reward of controlling ourselves in this world. We look ahead, not in a dream-world, but to the next world. We can accept the suffering of a moment as we gaze upon eternal joy.

Blessed are the gentle; they shall have the earth for their heritage.

If there is one area in which our Memory and Imagination can go out of control, it is the area of anger. All our anger seems justified, but most of the time it is not. Our Memory can recall past injuries that are twenty years old; our imagination pictures the scene and embellishes it with every recollection. We can become angry and hateful in the present moment because of something that happened long ago. Worse than that, we can live, and continue to live for years, in that past moment of anger. It can warp our souls and harden our hearts until we become the very thing we hate.

We can even use Scripture to substantiate our anger by quoting passages out of context. And then we go our way with a false sense of security, while we forget many other passages of Scripture that tell us to be patient, gentle, and to do good to those who hate us.

We become attached to living in our hateful little world, and smug in our own complacency. And suddenly one morning we wake up to realize we are all alone in our little world. We are without friend or foe. We have been unable to love enough to have a friend, or courageous enough to take a stand on anything that would create an enemy.

But Hope comes along and tells us that if we control our tempers, anger, past resentments and bitterness, every human being on earth will be a friend. Even enemies who render us the service of giving us the opportunity to forgive, have, in the act of offending, added jewels to our crown.

Hope keeps our Memory and Imagination from harboring resentments and gives us the assurance that no matter how dark things seem to be, our little boat is being guided by the hand of a loving and omnipotent Father.

It gives us a light heart in regard to disturbing occurrences and helps us to see God behind everything that happens.

Yes, the whole world will be our heritage if we can keep it where it belongs—on the outside of us. Then only will our innermost being be at its peak to give the world its best.

Blessed are those who mourn; they shall be comforted.

Jesus was not only speaking of compassion for those in sorrow, but He was speaking of all those who repent of their sins. The feeling of sorrow for past sins brings down upon us the comfort of God. This kind of sorrow is born of a deep repentance for having offended God, who has done nothing but good to us every moment of our lives.

This kind of mourning is unselfish. It is centered on God. But how many of us possess this kind of sorrow? Our Memory is filled with a sorrow for past sins, but it is born of guilt, not of love. We are not so much concerned with offending a loving Father as we are afraid of punishment. Sometimes our motives for sorrow are lower than a fear of punishment. We are ashamed to think we could commit such a sin, and if that sin is public, our guilt torments us even more. All of this kind of guilt is selfish and deprives God of glory.

There is no sin, or combination of sins, greater than the Infinite Mercy of God, and our sorrow must be God-centered and not self-centered.

This is the area where our Imagination and Memory can create havoc if we are not careful. We must put into practice the Virtue of Hope that the Lord has given us in order to control these faculties.

Guilt over past sins can create a shadow of doom and un-easiness every moment of our lives. The past can torture us with feelings of guilt so great that God becomes a terrible judge in our minds, and all the fatherly and loving attributes of God are smothered beneath the smoldering fire of fear and despair.

We have a good example of the right and wrong way of using the memories of past sins in Peter and Judas.

Since denial is a form of betrayal, and betrayal is a form of denial, we can say that both Peter and Judas denied and betrayed Our Lord. Though both fell, each reacted to his fall in a different way.

Peter rose to the level of Hope and was comforted by the Lord Himself. Judas sank deeper and deeper into his Memory and Imagination and despaired; he refused to rise above himself to God.

The remembrance of Peter's sin made him humble and dependent upon God's Mercy. The remembrance of Judas' sin centered itself on it's hideousness, and he despaired.

Peter wept bitterly because he had offended such a good Master, and that Goodness made him throw himself into the open arms of Infinite Mercy.

Judas screamed at the Pharisees that he had betrayed innocent blood, but his emphasis was on himself and on what he had done. He was disturbed over his conscience but not over His Lord. He had failed in a cheap business deal and his only thought was to return the money.

Peter's Memory brought back to him his sin, but Hope used it as a rung in his ladder to God. He was sure of his Master's forgiveness because his Master was God. All his life Peter benefited by that fall as he threw himself more and more into the one thing necessary in this life — to serve God. His fall was used to protect him from pride, and with a humble heart he was capable of doing great things for the Kingdom.

Judas, however, centered all his sorrow on himself and it ended in a remorse devoid of Hope. His Memory and Imagination took such a hold on him that he could not believe in the Mercy of God. He had lived so long on an emotional level that he was without Hope, and finally despaired.

Although we may not totally despair as Judas did, many of us waste precious time living over past sins and permitting the sorrow for those sins to grow into an agonizing remorse that fills our souls with sadness.

Peter had Hope and never denied his Master again. Judas lost Hope, and destroyed himself. We must use all our past regrets as opportunities for greater things, because they have taught us to depend on God and not on ourselves.

Blessed are those who hunger and thirst for what is right; they shall be satisfied.

Jesus is telling us that when we seek to live a holy life, that desire will be satisfied. He is also telling us that our Memory and Imagination must hunger and thirst for God and His Perfections in order to be satisfied.

If we are content to feed these faculties only the husks of swine, we shall find ourselves starving in the midst of plenty. We can easily lose a hunger for God by rationalizing all our actions and finding excuses for not praying, reading spiritual books or studying Scripture.

Our Memory can recall only the things we feed it, and our Imagination can visualize only those things that fill our heart, for where our heart is there our treasure is also.

It is very important that we be discerning as to what we see and hear, for what we see and what we hear are like so many jars on the shelf of our Memory. Every so often we take a jar off of that shelf and look at it. If the jar is filled with spoiled food, and our Memory and Imagination are constantly fed that food, then they shall starve and become diseased.

A constant diet of dog food could never nourish a human body, and neither can a constant diet of worldly thoughts and desires nourish our Memory and Imagination that they may be satisfied.

Our Memory, made to the Image of the Father, must be fed by the food pleasing to Him. It can only grow strong when it is fed by the same source from which it came. We do God and ourselves a great injustice when we treat our Memory as if it were a garbage can ready to be filled with the refuse of this world.

We must make every effort to treat these faculties with the respect they deserve, for they render us a great service, and to mistreat them is to destroy ourselves.

It is in seeking for God, and remembering our past offenses and present weaknesses, that Hope manifests one of its beautiful qualities—that is—the ability to persevere, by zealously doing our part, knowing that God will do His part. We must be careful to read good books, listen and see those things that lift our minds to a higher level, and speak the words we would not be ashamed to say in His Presence.

Everything we hear and see is recorded in our Memory, ready to encourage or disturb us at any moment. If we hunger and thirst for the things of God, our Memory will be fed the bread of heaven and we shall be satisfied, for it will be filled with the food that lasts for all eternity.

Blessed are the merciful; they shall have mercy shown them.

The remembrance of past and present injuries, especially those that are unjust, are perhaps the most difficult to control.

If we have offended someone and they have responded with angry words, we can somehow accept it, if for no other reason than we have made someone we dislike miserable.

But if someone does or says something that we feel is undeserved or unjust, then we store it in our Memory—in a very special corner. We call that corner "just anger." We almost pride ourselves in justifying our anger by telling ourselves and everyone else that it is right and true.

In the meantime, our Memory is becoming more and more saddened by what it is being fed, and our Imagination builds up a case against the person that is so convincing that severity and injustice replace mercy and compassion. We become so wrapped up in our own injuries that we speak of nothing

215

but truth and justice, and in justifying ourselves we refuse to forgive and forget.

It is so easy to blame others for our failure to see God's Will in everything. It takes *little* effort to see the injustice of every offense hurled at us. Our passions rise up to meet every occasion, and the thought of controlling them — by recalling the words of Jesus to be merciful in the same way that mercy has been rendered to us — is pushed into the background as being unreal.

We seemed possessed by the desire to call a spade a spade, and take pleasure in rehashing old injuries — like a knight in armor recalling his victories.

Yes, the world must know we have been injured — and this somehow takes away the pain. But what a great price for such little comfort. Each time we relive a past injury, it gnaws at our hearts and takes away a little more love. And, suddenly, we find ourselves cold, suspicious, unforgiving, and full of self-pity.

Jesus realized this when He told us to forgive seventy times seven times a day. Without forgiveness on our part, our Memory and Imagination are squeezed in the small area of self, unable to breathe the fresh air of love and freedom.

It is as if those faculties were compressed in a small jar, with the lid of hate so tight that it creates a vacuum of selfishness and spiritual death in our souls. Our reasoning powers are held captive, and our Wills become entrenched in the line of least resistance. It is then that we are tossed to and fro like a ship on a stormy sea.

What ability we possess to look at the situation objectively is lost in the maze of confusion constantly being stirred up by uncontrolled emotions.

Here again, Hope comes to the rescue. Hope gives us the assurance that it is not important to be positive of who hurt who and for what reason. It is only important that we seize the opportunity to imitate Jesus.

Hope does not take away the hurt, because being hurt isn't always the most difficult part. The difficult part of every offense is not so much the offense as the inability on our part to see any good reason for being offended. Of what purpose are enemies, insults, persecutions, and difficult personalities?

Here is where Hope elevates us to a higher level, for it assures us that even though we have failed, or been insulted, it has all passed through the mind of God and bears the stamp of His approval. For, how can I be merciful or forgiving if there is no one to forgive? Hope, again, sees opportunities rather than injuries, and it develops within our souls a beautiful spirit of merciful understanding—an understanding of poor, weak, fallen human nature.

So dear is a merciful heart to God, that it brings down upon its Memory and Imagination a calm and serenity undreamed of before. The soul can truly pray for and do good to its enemies as Jesus asked, because its faculties are free.

God Himself will justify the soul, either in this life or in the next, so it need not put its Memory and Imagination into a tail spin as it acts out the part of judge, prosecutor, and jury.

Blessed are the pure in heart; they shall see God.

Purity of heart is a broad subject and includes many facets of daily living. It means having God first in our lives. It means a clean mind, and it means having high spiritual goals and values.

Here again our Memory and Imagination can build up or completely destroy our union with God. We mentioned before how Jesus warned us about having lust in our hearts, "If a man looks at a woman lustfully, he has already committed adultery with her in his heart" (Matt. 5:28). He also told us that where our hearts were we would also find our treasure.

This is an indication of how much emphasis Jesus put upon the emotions as being a source of harm if they are not kept under control.

People who feed their Memory and Imagination on X-rated movies and bad books are slowly committing spiritual suicide. The unfortunate part of it all is the fact that since their feelings are involved they are not aware of the danger.

It is similar to the poor people who were on the Titanic. They were eating, drinking, and dancing as they came closer and closer to a giant iceberg that was ready to tear away the secure deck beneath their dancing feet. Suddenly, the fun was over. Reality met them face to face over the icy water.

And so it will be with those who use the marvelous faculties of Memory and Imagination as garbage cans, whose odor is obnoxious to everyone except the owners. They become so obsessed with feelings that they cannot see the glacier of ice tearing away all the love of God they ever had. Though they often speak of love, it is merely a flicker on a very dark night.

Lust is not the only vice that can possess a man's heart. Worldly pursuits for the sake of personal glory can also destroy our hearts. Man can misuse his Imagination and never be satisfied with the possessions he has already accumulated. His mind can be so filled with greed for things, money, glory and honor that he will lie, cheat, and steal to obtain them.

He imagines himself doing great things, and while he struggles he prays for help from God as he makes all sorts of promises as to what he will do for God once he has become rich and influential.

But his promises, like his dreams, are imaginary. They are merely the trick of an overworked Imagination ready to con even God. Lies are born in the Imagination, and if they are stored in the Memory, they become real.

Jesus told the Pharisees one day that they were like their father, the devil, who is the father of lies. They were proud men whose Memory and Imagination had puffed them up to the point where they began to believe they were the greatest of men.

An overworked Imagination can make our whole life a perpetual lie. We can live in a world of make-believe, never facing truth or reality—always trying to be someone we're not.

Hope lets us rise above all this fantasy by bringing to mind that no matter how beautiful or loving we desire things to be in this world, it is as nothing compared to what is to come. It gives us the courage to put forth the effort we need to overcome the lethargy that overpowers us and makes us dream of building castles without laying a stone.

Hope puts our hearts on a higher plane and permits us to persevere as we strive for a pure heart in thought and in deed.

Thoughts and desires may pester us like gnats in a swamp, but Hope blows a gentle breeze that keeps everything that is not of God, away from our hearts and souls. He has shown us the Way, and we attach our Memory and Imagination to the anchor of Hope, that they may stand still and firm during the storms of life.

Blessed are the peacemakers: they shall be called sons of God.

The Lord did not say that those who have peace are blessed, but those who *make* peace. Surely we are blest by God when we have peace, but the good God was telling us that there is an effort needed: we must be peacemakers within our own souls.

We must *make* peace, which is indicative of effort on our part. Peace is not the end result of everything in perfect order, with nothing to disturb us. If we are to make peace, it means that peace ordinarily is not our portion.

Peace is like anything else we make. We have an idea, a plan, material, and effort, and with this combination we succeed in making anything from a cake to an office building.

Because each person has a different temperament, with its inherent virtues and faults, each one of us must make peace in a different way. But no matter what that temperament may be, it is certain that all of us must keep our Memory and Imagination under control.

People lose peace over past sins, offenses, failures, and unfulfilled dreams. Fear of the future also causes a loss of peace, fear of illness, age, financial loss, and beauty.

It is so easy to see how important Hope is in our lives. God has given this uplifting virtue to us to calm our fears, to put a reason behind every unexplainable tragedy, to give us joy, to put Him above everything, and to realize we are merely pilgrims traveling Home, and these unpleasant occurrences in life are only part of the journey.

When we put our heart and soul into things, we live in a perpetual fear of losing them, and we experience a kind of vacuum at the very thought of being stripped of them. And yet, this very stripping is part of the growing process of Hope in our hearts. We are being shown, in a very graphic way, that everything in this world is passing—so many reminders that thus passes the glory of this world.

When we permit our Imagination to rebel and our Memory to bring back past glory, our souls are in constant turmoil, torn by what we want to be and what we are.

We must make peace between these truths—what we were, what we wanted to be, and what we are. Once Hope succeeds in doing this, we have peace. Hope puts all our desires in God who is everlasting and does not change. It makes us face reality with joy. It sees everything in the light of Eternity. Past sins are used to maintain humility, not despair. Past glory is used to maintain confidence, not pride. Past failures are used as guideposts of our abilities, not as stepping stones to discouragement.

Hope has the ability to use everything—good, bad, and indifferent—as opportunities for greater holiness. It is ever vibrant and ingenious in keeping our poor souls above ourselves and raising us to a higher level.

Yes, we make peace in our own lives, and in the lives of others, by ever seeking to bring good out of evil, doing all in our power to raise our neighbor above those things that hamper his peace, having courage to change the things that can be changed, while having hope that others will change the things we cannot change.

Hope does not pretend that a particular situation is not serious, neither is it flippant or flighty, refusing to face reality. Hope rouses our Memory and Imagination to *complete* reality—seeing both visible and invisible causes and remedies.

Without Hope, we see only one side of a situation—the miserable side; but with Hope we see also the good side. We see reasons, solutions—and we possess more and more assurance that God will make all things well.

St. Paul lost his peace one day, and every bit of Hope he ever had seemed to be gone. Everything was pressing in upon him and the future suddenly looked hopeless. He called this darkness of soul, "an angel of Satan" (2 Cor. 12:7).

The man who had spoken so eloquently on fighting the good fight, being zealous for God's honor and glory, loving enemies no matter what they did, and rejoicing to be found worthy to suffer something for the Kingdom—yes, *this* man became so depressed that he could not practice what he preached.

He had always been strong; he could always see the solution to other people's problems; he could see God's hand in their persecutions; and he could see clearly how God brought good out of evil; but this day, he saw nothing but darkness, and the strong Paul became very weak.

It was something he had not experienced before, and three times He asked God to deliver him from this feeling of failure and depression.

The answer he received was not the one he expected. His Memory and Imagination had successfully brought back all the sufferings of the past and had projected worse things in the future. There was only one solution to such a problem, and that was—deliverance. The suffering and persecution must stop, or he could go no further.

And then Jesus answered his prayer and said to him, "My grace is enough for you: my power is at its best in weakness" (2 Cor. 12:9). Now, Paul had a whole new concept of holiness. It was not becoming strong in himself, but in using God's grace in weakness that would make him holy.

No matter what his Memory and Imagination told him, no matter how dark the future, no matter how weak he was, he would be strong through God's grace and not through his own herculean strength.

In fact, his very weakness was the foundation upon which God would accomplish greater things. It was through God's strength that Paul would continue to work, despite the insults, hardships, persecutions, agonies, and his own weakness (2 Cor. 12:10).

He would use these heretofore hindrances as objects of Hope. He would boast that he suffered and was weak so that God's Power in him would be glorified.

But what was this power that would help him overcome discouragement, sadness, and depression?

What kind of power was more manifest in the midst of misery than in happiness?

What kind of power would calm his Memory and Imagination and enable him to rise above to peace and serenity?

What kind of paradox was this—power dependent upon weakness, and weakness bearing the fruit of power?

To our human way of reasoning, all the hardships Paul was experiencing were anything but graces. He could see no good in his miseries.

His Memory and Imagination rebelled against a constant diet of frustration, even though Hope kept him from despair.

The Lord was teaching His Apostle in gradual stages. Paul's zeal had caused him to persecute the Christians, and that same zeal pushed him forward to overcome every force once he was converted. His whole attitude towards life situations, good and bad, had to change. Faith demanded that he begin to think like Jesus, and to see everything in the light of Faith: he must live on a Faith level.

His convictions were strong, and he went out to make converts with the same zeal with which he had persecuted them. His emotions were on a high level as he spoke to anyone who would listen, yet there was something Paul still had to learn, and that was — to live by Faith.

The man of emotions had to see God and God's people in a different way. He was to learn how to use his emotions to express his feelings, but not to live in them — he was to live in Jesus — in Faith — in his Understanding. And this way of living was best reached by weakness.

We will look at this new way of living and thinking, and see how we can be like Jesus.

OUTLINE 3
Sharing His Nature through Baptism

The "Memory" is given Hope — to keep it from despair, discouragement and sadness, and to protect it from presumption.

The "Understanding" is given Faith—to raise it above itself to see invisible reality.

The "Will" is given Supernatural Love—to unite itself to God in everything it accomplishes.

Second Key: *Understanding & Faith*

Man's power to reason raises him to a level next to the Angels. He not only knows *who* he is, but *what* he is, and this knowledge gives him dignity and self-confidence. He does not run aimlessly through life, guided by instinct.

He not only knows when it is time to eat, but he can grow, produce, and prepare what he eats.

He not only responds to his name; he knows the personality, talents, sins, weaknesses, failures, and successes of the person behind that name—himself.

And so he reasons out everything that presents itself to him. He possesses an intellectual life—a life invisible to another man's eye but very real and active. Only a small portion of one's thoughts are made visible by gestures, actions, or words. A whole world of calm and storm, fear and courage, darkness and light, are experienced in that inner realm of intellect.

Battles are fought—some are won and some are lost—in that inner sanctum. And we can say in all truth that ninety-five percent of a man is within while only five percent is visible to other men.

The intellect is a faculty that is sublime and makes us master of every other form of life in this world. But unless it, too, is elevated to a higher level, it may accomplish great things in the eyes of the world but it will always be limited in its effect upon mankind. It must have something to increase its capabilities and capacity. It must have Faith to accept God.

Faith keeps alive the realization that there is a God. I have the power to bring that God into our very souls, for it is a grace, given by God's own Spirit. It makes us think like God.

Faith in Jesus elevates our reasoning powers to a level of light undreamed of before. The Understanding is no longer dependent upon visible things alone; it penetrates and fathoms *invisible* things—things of God—things that eye has not seen nor ear heard.

Now, we need no longer be tossed to and fro by emotions and forces that our poor souls are unable to cope with; we can see things as He sees them.

Faith, added to our Understanding, sets our souls free into those regions where the air is so pure that only the unburdened and unhampered can breathe.

Our intellect, darkened and hampered by passions, clouded by ignorance, and tied down with pride, can now roam the vault of Heaven and speak to God face to face through Faith.

Now, our souls have a place to abide in this valley of tears. St. Paul found this hidden place when he said, "There are three things that last: Faith, Hope, and Love" (1 Cor. 13:13). Our Memory and Imagination are lifted from the depths by Hope; our Understanding is raised into Heaven by Faith; and our Will is united to God by Love.

We are to be renewed, and St. Paul reminded us of this when he said to the Ephesians, "You must give up your old way of life; you must put aside your old self which gets corrupted by following illusory desires. Your mind must be renewed by a spiritual revolution, so that you can put on the new self that has been created in God's way — in the goodness and holiness of the truth" (Eph. 4:22-24).

Jesus said that He was the Truth, and our Understanding must be renewed in Him. This Spiritual Revolution must take place as we renew our minds and elevate them with the gifts

God has given us. It is often painful, always takes effort, planning, and prayer — but the change is well worth the time and sacrifice: we shall be brought to the very Heart of God in this life and eternal glory in the next life.

Faith in Christ Jesus elevates our Understanding so that through it, as St. Paul says, we are made "sons of God.... All baptized in Christ, you have all clothed yourselves in Christ" (Gal. 3:26-27).

Our finite mind, so limited by what it sees, needs Faith to lift it to those regions where its contact with Infinite Goodness *changes its way of thinking* and sheds light when everything is in darkness.

We often look at Faith as something abstract — an acceptance of a revelation that we cannot fully comprehend. But to Paul and the first Christians it was much more — it was something alive. It *changed their lives*, their *minds*, their *hearts* — it made them new men.

We can imagine Paul as he wrote to the Corinthians and said, "From now onwards, therefore, we do not judge anyone by the standards of the flesh. Even if we did once know Christ in the flesh that is not how we know Him now. And for anyone who is in Christ, there is a *new creation*; the old creation is gone, and now the new one is here (1 Cor. 5:16-17).

It is this new creation, brought about by Faith, in our Understanding, that we must study, look at, and grow in, if we are to be renewed.

Our Understanding is renewed by our Faith in Jesus. This means more than an acceptance of Him as Savior. It also means, as quoted above by St. Paul, an acceptance of Him as the Word of God, begotten of the Father. That Word must ever dwell in our Understanding—it must be a source of living water and a never-ending source of light. To live by those words is Faith.

Jesus mentioned the direction our Understanding must take when He said, "If anyone loves Me, he will keep My word and My Father will love him and We shall come and make Our home with him."

"Those who do not love Me, do not keep My words."

"If you remain in Me, and My words remain in you, you may ask what you will and you shall get it" (John 14:23-24; 15:7).

Jesus went so far as to explain to us that it is that very word that the Father uses to prune us. After explaining to His Apostles that the Father would prune them so they would bear more fruit, He told them how this was done. He said, "You are pruned already, by means of the word that I have spoken to you" (John 15:3).

The words of Jesus living in our Understanding and stored in our Memory will keep our souls in peace. Jesus was always astounded when His apostles lacked faith, when they so quickly forgot His words and signs and yielded to fear. They forgot to recall His words and live by them.

Jesus demanded Faith from everyone—a Faith that springs from humility. We must be humble to accept everything Jesus told us. Our Understanding creates doubts in our hearts because it cannot rise above its own limitations. But when it is filled with Faith, nothing is impossible, because it judges everything by the words of Jesus and not by its own words.

It may be well for us to look at Scripture and see how those who followed Jesus practiced and grew in Faith.

Since sin seems to be one thing that drags our souls down, we will look first at a sinner and see how Faith guided her through the depths.

Jesus was invited to a dinner at the house of one of the leading Pharisees. He had been invited to the feast, not out of love, but merely out of curiosity. They wanted to observe this young Rabbi at close range.

A woman came in, whose soul was overburdened with sin. Her Memory and Imagination must have tormented her for years with guilt, only to drive her deeper into greater sins, in order to forget those of the past. She no doubt had heard about the gentle Master who understood and forgave.

What struggles must her soul have experienced when she first thought of asking forgiveness. Her Memory must have brought back her past sins with great rapidity and her Imagination embellished them until she seemed surrounded with the horror of despair. But surely these faculties would not stop there. She had lived so long in her emotions that they would fight for control. They would picture to her a bleak future without the sins that had given her so much pleasure. But they would hide the misery that had accompanied every moment of that sinful past.

Her poor soul must have cried out in the agony of death as it strove to free itself from the depths of despair.

We do not know when this woman heard the Master, but what she heard gave her a spark of Hope, and that spark was all she needed to set off the fire of love.

No matter what her Memory and Imagination told her, she would hang on to His words of Mercy, Love, and Compassion.

She would replace the remembrance of her sins with the parable of the prodigal son. When her Reason told her that God would never forgive her sins because they were so hideous, she would remember the woman who was caught in adultery. Those words rang in her ears, "Has no one condemned you? Neither do I condemn you: go away, and don't sin anymore" (John 8:10-11).

As she struggled, rays of light broke through the darkness, and her Understanding began to lift itself out of the mire of filth and to breathe in the fresh air of peace. It, too, had to change. Her Memory told her it was hopeless, and her Understanding told her it was impossible. But the sound of His Voice planted the seed of Faith, and the look of compassion on His Face gave her Hope. She began to throw off the human reasoning of her faculties and to live in the unknown regions of the Spirit—a region in which she knew little but understood much. She longed for deliverance, and the sudden realization that He would forgive, made her seek Him out.

She heard that He had been invited to the house of the Pharisee, and disregarding all human respect she went into the house. She looked neither to the right nor left but made straight for the Master.

She knelt at His feet, and when she touched them, Mercy flowed out to her as healing did to the woman who touched the hem of His garment. Her many sins were forgiven; her struggle with her human faculties was rewarded; she was free. The relief was so great that she began to cry, and her tears fell copiously on His feet. She had nothing to dry them with except her beautiful long hair. The human beauty she had used to attract men, she would use to wipe away her tears of contrition. She would renew her whole being — body and soul — she would change — she would rise above the depths into the heights.

She would not destroy her emotions; she would redirect them into the paths of God. She would glorify His Mercy for all Eternity.

Everyone in the dining hall looked at her with disdain — everyone but Jesus. He knew her sins but He also knew her struggle, effort, and desires. She believed in His Words of Mercy, and she was there because of that belief.

She refused to believe or live in her own words; she would live by His words. She did not make the mistake most of us make. No, she put aside her finite reasoning and her unbridled imagination and believed His words.

Jesus looked at her and said, "Your sins are forgiven. Your faith has saved you; go in peace" (Luke 7:48-50).

We don't often think of faith in relation to the forgiveness of sins, and yet, the lack of faith is the real cause of so many guilt complexes — complexes that cripple and destroy lives and happiness.

Sometimes, past sins return to haunt us because we may have offended others, but the words of Jesus in which faith is grown, tell us that God can and will bring good out of evil. If we have offended someone and expressed our contrition by apologizing, and the offended person refuses to forgive, our faith tells us to leave it to Jesus. He will take care. We have only to pray for that person and keep our hearts free of resentment. That is Faith.

We see from the Gospels that all those who sought forgiveness were what we would term "big sinners." There is nothing anyone could do today that these men and women had not done.

The difference between them and ourselves is not in the hideousness or enormity of sin, but in our faith. They heard Him say, "It is not the healthy who need the doctor, but the sick. Go and learn the meaning of the words, 'What I want is mercy, not sacrifice.' And indeed I did not come to call the virtuous but sinners" (Matt. 9:12-13).

These words took root in the souls of these sinners; they lived by them, and they were forgiven and freed. We, today, read them but prefer to live by our own words—the words born of a finite, unforgiving intellect, and the Truth is not in us—it is only in Jesus.

Because our Understanding is so limited, it is difficult to believe that God forgives and forgets. We tend to judge Him by our standards or worldly standards, and we forget that the wisdom of men is foolishness to God.

Jesus told us that as we measure out mercy, mercy will be measured out to us. These are living words that must be lived and experienced, not just read and forgotten. Our human Understanding cannot be permitted to rationalize justice in regard to our neighbor, and mercy in our own regard.

As it is with mercy, so it is with every other virtue. We must live our lives by His example and words, and this is to live by Faith, because our own reasoning and emotions are often contrary to His reasoning and Will.

We can see this in the explanation Jesus gave to His Apostles in regard to the parable of the sower. He told them that "when anyone hears the word without understanding, the evil one comes and carries off what was sown in his heart" (Matt. 13:19). In other words, the Good News was stored in their Memory (heart) but never reached their Understanding. They never studied it, reasoned it out, or began to live by it, so it was easy for the evil one to push it out of their minds completely by substituting other thoughts, imaginings and desires.

He continued, "The one who received it on patches of rock is the one who hears the word and welcomes it with joy. But he has no root in him, he does not last; let some trial come, or some persecution on account of the word and he falls away at once" (Matt. 13:20-21). Here we have someone who has not only stored the word in his Memory but found great joy in it. But his joy is purely emotional; his acceptance of the word in the first place was because of its emotional quality. Being loved by a Great God gave him a feeling of Hope, joy, and security.

This kind of man judges the efficacy of the word entirely by his feelings, and he will do all in his power to keep those feelings on a high level. This kind of piety can be called in truth "the opium of the people." God is used as a kind of tranquilizer or anesthetic to blot out reality and life.

Because the Word never reaches the Understanding that has been elevated by Faith, this kind of man falls away as soon as some trial or persecution comes along. The reason for this is that any kind of suffering, in any form, takes away his feelings.

His Understanding, still operating on a natural level, can see no reason for trials or the cross. It is pure nonsense to him because in his emotional world he has imagined the trials God would send him. In these trials, he comes through in a blaze of glory, and the thought of carrying his cross, and following the Lord, has in his mind become just another level of emotion, not a quiet sacrifice for God.

Unfortunately, or perhaps, fortunately, the trials that come his way may be quite different from the ones his human reasoning has projected. He is given an opportunity to rise to the faith level—by accepting the trials he does not understand. Because his love for God is shallow, even his sufferings must be tailor-made and specially built to fit the shallow water in which his boat sails, and so he cannot accept the trials he does not understand.

Consequently, when any suffering that he cannot explain comes his way, or that he cannot endure with glory and attention, or understand its place in his life, he falls away from his new found faith. He tried to put faith in his Memory and Imagination level, and it did not fit. Like a fish out of water, it died.

Jesus goes on to tell us of another type of person: the one who received the word among thorns. He said that such a man "hears the word, but the worries of this world and the lure of riches choke the word—and he produces nothing" (Matt. 13:22).

Now here is where a great percentage of mankind live, as far as their life with God is concerned. This is the area in which our souls are in the greatest danger. The reason is that both worry and the desire for riches seem to be the things that are part and parcel of daily life. There is hardly a person alive who does not have a legitimate reason to worry. Neither are there very many of us who do not think that a more comfortable way of life would be to our advantage.

When the Lord described this category of mankind, He pulled out the comfortable rug of excuses on which we have stood so long. To our dismay, He pulled it out from under us almost with an air of disgust, and said bluntly that we "produce nothing."

At least the man in the first category did not understand the word, and the one in the second received it for a time, but those of us who permit worry and worldly ambitions to choke out the word, seem to be more deliberate in our actions and more aware of our choices. We *permit* them to take over.

When our Memory and Imagination are in complete control, we begin to rationalize our worries and ambitions until they appear legitimate and necessary; then it is that they begin to choke His word and revelations out of our minds.

We become so absorbed in what appears to be right and good that we can keep ourselves distressed our entire lives. We look for solutions to our problems and avenues of escape, but we never seek the answer in God. He is so far away and of another world that our relationship with Him is unreal, and we doubt both His knowledge and care of us.

Why do we insist on the need to worry? We go so far as to call it "concern," but down deep in our hearts we know it is not so much concern as a lack of confidence in the Father's Providence.

To talk over our problems with God is a form of prayer. It is also an occasion to *empty* our Memory and Imagination of the superfluities that have accumulated.

The Lord wants us to talk over our problems, disappointments, heartaches, and sufferings with Him. And in this area, nothing is too small or too great. He is deeply interested in each part of our lives, and wants to share in everything that concerns us. So it is His Will that we run to Him with all our needs.

To speak of them to God is to lift them from our minds and put them into His Mind. But here is the point where most of us fail. After we have given them to God, we immediately take them back, and the burden becomes heavier and more unbearable. Our Memory and Imagination, aided by our natural reasoning, tells us that we must really solve this problem by ourselves.

It is true that we must often plan moves that help solve these problems, but that belongs to the action category. To worry, however, is not to do — it is to do nothing but think negative thoughts — thoughts that drain all hope from our Memory and all Faith from our Understanding.

Indeed, worry chokes the word from our minds and leaves us to ourselves. And though we cry to God for help, we refuse to let go of our problems. We hang on to them like a security blanket that eventually smothers us to death.

The lure of riches is another danger that is cloaked with an air of legitimacy. Jesus used the word "lure" because, like artificial bait enticing a fish, riches entice men to reach out for false hopes and pleasures.

A fish, looking at an artificial lure dangling from the hook of a fisherman, is under the impression that what it sees is real, appetizing, and satisfying. The fisherman has gone to a great expense to create this impression and he is satisfied to sit for hours dangling his lure, waiting for some unsuspecting fish to bite.

A bystander on the shore watching such a scene is fully aware of what is about to take place—so is the fisherman. The only one oblivious of the real consequences of his next move is the fish. And it only finds out too late.

Jesus is the bystander on the shore of life, and He is telling us to stay away from the lure dangling from the reel of the evil one.

We must rise above worry and unnecessary possessions in order to keep our Memory clean and our Understanding clear enough to hear His word and live by it. If we do not, we will produce nothing but anxiety and frustration.

It is in Matthew's account of the sower that we find an interesting addition. He says, "And the one who received the seed in rich soil is the man who hears the word and understands it; he is the one who yields a harvest and produces now a hundredfold, now sixty, now thirty" (Matt. 13:23).

Jesus is telling us very plainly that it is on the Understanding-Faith level that we produce fruit, and we do this in proportion as we understand the word because we do not always produce the same amount of fruit. The word "now" indicates that there are times in our life when we believe His word and live by it and then we produce a hundredfold.

But there are other times when, even though we understand, we still hesitate and draw back. Then it is that we produce sixty-fold.

And then, there are other times when circumstances and our finite minds join forces and tell us that this problem or difficulty is impossible, and that even God cannot help. But, somehow, we hang on to a thread of Faith and manage to survive and bear thirty-fold fruit.

What makes us draw back and permit our human reasoning to take over our lives so completely? There seems to be only one answer to that question, and the answer is—a lack of humility.

If we cannot fully understand the Mysteries of God, we will not accept them, and when we do not accept them we cannot make them a part of our daily life. They become mere "beliefs" that we reluctantly accept because we need some kind of crutch, or we reject because they are above our own Reasoning.

Sometimes we play games, and accept some revelations while rejecting others that do not suit us. And we use that very reasoning power, by which we accept some revelations, to rationalize ourselves out of believing other mysteries on Faith alone.

For example, we know God can do all things, but our human reasoning tells us that this time He can't or won't.

We know God loves us, but our intellect cannot comprehend His personal love and attention so we become just another pebble on the beach.

We know that God is present everywhere, and especially present in our souls through grace, but since our Understanding cannot fully comprehend "how," we go our way as if He were nowhere.

We know there is a God because every effect must have a cause, but since our Understanding cannot explain a Power that is Pure Spirit, we prefer to call Him "Nature."

To give credit for all creation to "Mother Nature" is to bring God down to our sense level where we can compete with Him on an equal basis. But the basis is not one of equality but pride on our part. We manage to keep ourselves from ever rising to the level of Faith because we insist on boxing ourselves inside the narrow limits of our own minds.

We remember when He said we should forgive seventy times seven times a day. But we apply this only when we are the ones to be forgiven. Our human Reasoning tells us that this is impossible when someone offends us that often.

We remember when He said we should love our enemies and do good to them. But our Intellect tells us that we cannot love anyone who hates us—it is asking too much—it is unreasonable.

We remember when He said that we should love each other in the same way He loves us. But the thought of this Commandment is perhaps one of the few times that we acknowledge an important truth, because we completely dismiss the Commandment, saying, "We can't do that because God loves with an Infinite Love and we are only finite." Yes, we are finite, but we admit that truth at the wrong time and the wrong place.

We remember how He spoke of His Father in Heaven and that He was going there to prepare a place for us. But our human Understanding rationalizes us right out of Heaven because it refuses to rise above itself to the region of God and Pure Spirits—a place where Faith alone can enter during this earthly sojourn.

Human reasoning can calm our emotions for awhile, and though they bear the fruit of self-control, it is self-centered — control for the sake of human respect — to be seen by men. What is thought to be control only drives us to a more subtle form of selfishness and pride. It does not change us into Jesus; it merely controls our emotions, leaving our Understanding still on the natural level.

Only when our Understanding is elevated by Faith in Jesus do we change and become sons of God and heirs to the Kingdom. Faith gives us a new birth. It puts away our old way of thinking and adopts a new way. We put on the mind of Christ, as St. Paul urged us to do.

As Christians, we not only believe; we think and live by those beliefs. We reason and understand by His standards, not ours or the world's. We see events, people, disappointments, trials, and suffering in a new light. We not only have Faith but we *live* by Faith.

Living in this light, we are unburdened and free to breathe the fresh air of joy and freedom, because we have already begun to live in Him.

Heaven is wherever God is, and though we live in a physical world, we also live in a spiritual one. The physical is outside of us, and passing; the spiritual is within us and everlasting. Since we are composed of body and soul, there must be harmony between these two lives. One must help the other towards happiness in this life and the next.

If we put an unbalanced emphasis on the spiritual, we run the risk of becoming cold, stoic, and unconcerned. If we put too much emphasis on the physical, we become selfish and greedy.

We see in Jesus a perfect balance between the physical and spiritual, and it is this harmony that we seek. Our passions and desires must be subject to our intellectual powers so that we are not tossed to and fro like a rudderless boat on a stormy sea. On the other hand, if we ignore the physical part of our nature we run the risk of killing the old man instead of renewing him and having a rebirth.

To be born again in the Spirit is to live on a supernatural plane. We must point out that the word "super" means above, exalted. So we take what we have—human nature—and with the virtues of Faith, Hope, and Love, we raise what is and always will be human and finite, to a higher level—a level of participation into a life higher and more sublime than our own.

Though our human nature with all its inherent weaknesses is always with us, we can, calmly and consistently, raise it up to a higher and happier plane.

We notice in the parable of the sower that Jesus speaks of the "rich soil" into which the seed fell, to bear various quantities of fruit.

For soil to be rich in the properties necessary for a plentiful harvest, it needs fertilizer, and we must exert every effort to keep the ever-growing weeds down to a minimum.

And so it is with our souls. His Power is at its best in weakness. Our souls are rich in weaknesses that keep us constantly stirred up. We can use that rich soil as a garbage heap by piling sin upon sin, or we can keep the soil weeded and use the fertilizer of our weaknesses to grow lasting fruit for the Kingdom.

To our human nature, God has added the ingredients of Faith, Hope, and Love to produce a plentiful harvest. But if we do not put forth the effort to cultivate and weed it, the enemy will sow more and more weeds, and the rich soil will be drained of its ingredients and become sterile ground.

God is the Sower and we are the gardeners. He has sown the Virtue of Hope in our Memory, Faith in our Understanding, and Love in our Will. As good gardeners, we use our weaknesses to grow in virtue by pulling out the weeds of sin that lessen our fruit and mar the beauty of our garden. Jesus told us this when He said, "It is to the glory of My Father that you should bear much fruit, and then you will be My disciples" (John 15:8).

St. Paul realized this when he said he would make his weaknesses his special boast, so that the Power of Christ may stay over him (2 Cor. 12:9). He used his weaknesses to grow in the image of Jesus. He was careful, however, that those weaknesses did not bear the harvest of sin. His failures healed his pride and made him depend more upon God.

We come now to a facet of the Christian life that we find difficult to understand and harmonize: weaknesses and holiness — the ridiculous changed into the sublime — the very human becoming divine.

People in the past have sometimes depicted holy people as otherworldly, unemotional, indifferent, and untouched by human passions and weaknesses — super beings set aside by God to arrive at a supernatural state unattainable by the rest of mankind.

Nothing can be more false. The real difference is that they used these weaknesses, and we try to destroy them. We find, however, that as soon as we think we have overcome one weakness, it either crops up again or something else takes its place. Then we are discouraged and give up the fight as a hopeless cause.

We attempt to fight invisible foes and weaknesses with visible weapons, and that is often our first and last mistake.

When our Memory recalls some unpleasant past experience, we sit there as if we were in front of a television screen and enjoy the whole thing. We live and relive it until it is so blown out of proportion that we are enmeshed in a maze of fantasy.

To recall past offenses is a weakness of our human nature. Possessing that weakness is not what's wrong with us. The success or failure lies in how we handle it. And the way we handle it will determine how strong or weak that frailty will become.

If we consistently give in, that weakness will control us. If we overcome it, we will conquer it even though we may never destroy it.

It is not feeling anger that displeases God; it is giving in to anger and letting the sun go down on our anger that warps our soul (Eph. 4:26).

When the Holy Spirit told us not to let the sun go down on our anger He was giving us a plan. We must put our Memory at rest before we retire every night. We must look back at the day's events and forgive and forget, and if we can't forget, then look at the day through the eyes of Jesus.

We must accept the events of that day in the light of Faith. We must forgive and use the unpleasant to increase humility, and rejoice in the pleasant, for both are ordained or permitted by God for our good. This is where Faith plays such an important role in our lives.

A Christian *sees* everything in the light of Faith, and he *thinks* in the light of Faith. It is here that we prove whether we are Christian in name or in deed.

When God gave us a plan by telling us *what* to do, namely, not to let the sun go down on our anger, He also told us *how* to accomplish this effectively.

In the Gospel of St. Luke, Jesus said, "Be compassionate as Your Father is compassionate" (Luke 6:36). Many translations use the word "Merciful" but Mercy seems to be the fruit of Compassion, so we shall look at this passage and use the new translation to see how it fits in our daily life.

Compassion is a "feeling" that belongs to that faculty most concerned with the category of Memory and Imagination. It is not surprising then that Jesus has asked us to be compassionate as the Father is compassionate.

When we are compassionate we sympathize with our neighbor's weaknesses, and even though they offend us, we somehow understand. We are able to be objective and have an understanding heart, fully aware of our own weaknesses.

We must grow in the feeling of Compassion, because compassion must be substituted for uncontrolled anger, impatience, and an unforgiving heart.

Scripture says many times that Jesus had compassion on the multitudes or on sinners. He felt sorry for them for they were like sheep without a shepherd. The very word "compassion" gives us a kind and warm feeling.

We are not asked by Jesus to destroy our feelings. We are asked to *change* and *elevate* them. The virtue of Hope gives us courage to persevere through the maze of bad memories, and results in the feeling of well-being that we call joy.

But for the unpleasant incident that is not yet a Memory but very much in the present moment, we need Compassion to make us Merciful.

It is here at this point that Faith must bring us to that other step so necessary to preserve our determination to rise above the things of this world.

Jesus told us to be perfect as our heavenly Father is perfect. Hope, joy, and compassion belong to our "feelings" and they aid that part of our human nature in order to raise it above itself.

The word "perfect" is not at all related to exterior order or perfection, but to an elevation of our minds to a different level—a level in which perfection is more easily attained.

This is a spiritual level that we are encouraged to reach for, a level untouched by the feelings, which tend to drag us down to the animal level. We must realize that if we ignore our life with God, we run the risk of living an unrestrained life—a life directed only by our senses in much the same way as an animal is directed by instinct.

When we substitute and develop feelings of compassion for anger or hatred, we are calming our passions, but we are still operating on the lower level of the "senses." We must now add a new dimension and rise to the spiritual level of Faith and live by more perfect standards—purely spiritual standards—the same standards Our Father lives by—and that demands Faith.

As our senses and emotions are held more in control by substituting compassion, joy, and hope for dangerous emotions, we clear the way to elevate the "higher" faculties of our soul—the Understanding and Will.

As we speak of one faculty, it is often necessary to bring in one or two of the others for greater clarity. Though each faculty is different, they work together in such a close relationship that we are hardly conscious of their difference.

So far, then, we have been told by Jesus to be compassionate and perfect as the Father is compassionate and perfect. We also know that Jesus is the perfect image of the Father. That perfect Image has become Man to show us "how" and to tell us "what" to do.

To know what He did is historical knowledge, but to make it a part of our life by imitating Him is Faith. And the degree of Faith we have will be determined not by how much we know, but by how much we make Him a part of our life.

Here is where our human Understanding rebels—rebels because it is often rooted in pride. When we begin to deal with our Intellect and speak of supernatural standards, truths, and revelations, our human Understanding is at a disadvantage.

Our intellect is so dependent upon our senses and memory for the knowledge it defines and rationalizes, that it is at a loss when it is asked to deal with the purely spiritual. In the realm of the spiritual our senses fail us completely. And yet, we are asked by God, with the help of His Grace (not our senses), to rise to His level of perfection.

But Grace, too, is invisible, and so we are in need of something to enable us to comply with Divine commands on our level.

The quality that we need to accomplish this seemingly impossible task is Faith.

As our Memory is elevated by Hope, and developed by Compassion, so our Understanding is elevated by Faith and is developed by Humility and Meekness.

We have been given the gift of Faith, and Jesus has told us how to increase this gift. He said, "Learn from Me, for I am gentle and humble in heart, and you will find rest for your souls" (Matt. 11:29). To accept the revelations of Jesus, we must be humble and admit they are above us.

If we are not humble, doubt will cause unrest in our souls. The inability to solve the problem of pain and suffering causes unrest in our souls. The difficulty of accepting truths that are within our reason, and yet above that reason, causes unrest in our souls.

The desire and inability to eradicate poverty and disease causes unrest in our souls. The unexplainable reasons for all the heartache and disappointments in daily life cause unrest in our souls.

There are a multitude of things in life that all crowd in upon our Understanding, clamoring for explanations. But our reasoning power, unaided by Faith, cannot solve these problems or answer these questions.

So our Understanding must either rise above itself through Faith or it will be in a constant state of doubt and frustration. When it is unable to cope with unsolvable problems it will either pretend they are not there or manufacture some logical solution that does nothing but touch the surface.

So we find the scientist who refuses to believe in God, making up his own explanations for the mysteries his reason cannot understand. But somehow they never satisfy him or anyone else for too long.

We find a social worker, who sees poverty, sickness, and injustice, losing his faith in God because his Understanding cannot solve or aid such astronomical problems alone.

We see those who have been unjustly offended becoming bitter because their Understanding can see no reason for persecution.

And then there are those who sincerely try to lead good lives only to be visited by tragedy and misfortune. Their Understanding questions and sometimes rebels at the injustice of it all.

Truly, our Understanding, unaided by Faith, cannot cope with, live with, or endure, those multitudes of crises that plague our daily lives.

In the Old Testament, Faith was based on the Hope of a Savior. Now, our Faith is based on a belief in Jesus as Lord and our imitation of Him as God-Man.

We are saved by this kind of Faith because Jesus is its source. "It is in Him and through Him that we move and have our being" (Acts 17:28).

This kind of Faith has the power to *change* us into sons of God. But in this area we often put the cart before the horse by just affirming a belief that Jesus is Lord through lip service. We then attempt to prove our sincerity by good works, like giving to some charity.

Faith that produces nothing but empty words never reaches our Understanding. It has been merely a balm for a bad conscience and it produces nothing. It never changes us.

The kind of Faith Jesus wants us to have is the kind that changes our way of *thinking* and *acting*. It reasons on a higher plane and sees things in a totally different light than our human way of reasoning.

We have an example of this in the way the Apostles acted before and after Pentecost. In the Gospel of St. Mark we read where Jesus foretold Peter's denial and the other Apostles' flight in His time of need.

Jesus said to them, "You will all lose Faith.... However, after My Resurrection I shall go before you into Galilee" (Mark 14:27-28).

Peter's faith was not as strong as he thought it was. He confused his faith with his emotional love for Jesus and his admiration of His Power. Peter's reply to Jesus was, "Even if all lose faith, I will not."

Even Peter's Hope was not as yet elevated, for now he is presumptuous, and presumption is opposed to Hope.

Yes, though Peter thought he had everything an Apostle needed to persevere through the test, he soon found out it was all natural—all on the surface—he was not thinking like Jesus.

Peter's Hope and Faith were built on such an emotional level that even after Jesus predicted his denial, he still reiterated his allegiance by saying, "If I have to die with You, I will never disown You" (Mark 14:31).

The important lesson in this passage is not so much Peter's presumption as the statement from Jesus that they would *lose* their Faith that very night.

In telling the Apostles how they would lose their Faith, Jesus has told the rest of us what Faith is really all about.

We have said before that the Apostles lived on an emotional level. They could not stand the thought of His suffering, death, and departure, neither did they ever really hear, as He spoke of His Resurrection.

Jesus knew that as long as they lived on that level, His Cross would be a scandal to their human way of Understanding, and as a result, they would lose their Faith.

They had fulfilled only a part of the necessary requirements of Faith — a belief in Jesus as Son of God. They had yet to fulfill the most important requirement — to transform their Understanding to His way of Understanding.

One day when Jesus asked His Apostles who they thought He was, Peter said, "You are the Christ, the Son of the Living God" (Matt. 16:16). Jesus told Peter that the Father Himself revealed this to him.

Jesus looked at Peter and said, "You are Peter and on this Rock I will build My Church" (Matt. 16:18). Peter had a special revelation that gave him a realization that what appeared to be only a Man was truly God. He bore public witness to this fact and was rewarded with the *Keys of the Kingdom* by which he could loose or bind on earth and it would be so in Heaven.

This was a glorious moment for Peter and he reveled in it. Joy filled his heart every time he thought about that moment.

And then, a few days later, "Jesus began to make it clear to His disciples that He was destined to go to Jerusalem and suffer grievously at the hands of the elders, be put to death, and rise on the third day" (Matt. 16:21). Peter's Understanding rebelled at the thought. This would be a tragedy and something had to be done about it. What would become of this small band of followers if this were to happen? The Church would be destroyed before it ever began, without the Master.

These thoughts must have plagued Peter's mind until he could stand it no more. "Then, taking Him aside, Peter started to remonstrate with Him, 'Heaven preserve You, Lord,' he said, 'this must not happen to you'" (Matt: 16:22).

Jesus turned to the man who just a few days before proclaimed Him the Son of God, and said, "Get behind Me, Satan!

You are an obstacle in My path, because the way you think is not God's way but man's" (Matt. 16:23).

Peter made the first step in Faith—an acknowledgment of Jesus as Lord, but his Understanding, created to resemble the Son he professed, was not thinking in the same way as Jesus. It was too human. He had still to take the final step into Faith and put on the "mind of Christ" (1 Cor. 2:16).

He was thinking the way a man would think, not as God would think. He unwittingly became an obstacle and a tool of Satan in the Lord's path.

To change his way of thinking so drastically would take a great deal of humility on the part of Peter. He was not ready for such a step.

Peter and the rest of the Apostles had to learn by sad experience the consequences of a faith based on exterior signs alone.

It was only when Peter denied Jesus and the other disciples fled that they realized there was something missing in their Faith. It was much more than believing Jesus was Lord because of His works. It was to think as He thought, to see as He saw, and to do as He did.

The very failure to stay with Him in His time of need was used by them to keep them humble—humble enough to want to distrust their own Understanding and accept everything in the way He did.

Faith that does not lead to imitation in thought and deed is merely an acknowledgment of an historical fact, that Jesus is the Lord, but even Satan knows that. St. Paul put it beautifully when he said, "It would be a sign from God that He has given you the privilege not only of believing in Christ but of suffering for Him as well" (Phil. 1:29).

Yes, both parts of Faith are privileges from God, but the sign that we possess the gift of Faith is the ability to suffer for Him.

Knowing how distasteful such a sign would be to our human way of thinking, Paul encourages the Philippians to have a common purpose without conceit. They were to be self-effacing, thinking of other people's interests rather than their own.

He put the crowning touch on it all by saying,

> His state was divine,
> yet He did not cling
> to His equality with God but emptied Himself
> to assume the condition of a slave,

and became as men are; and being as all men are,
He was humbler yet
even to accepting death,
death on a Cross. (Phil. 2:6-8)

Yes, Faith is a gift, and it is a sign when we are willing to suffer something for Jesus. It develops by humbly giving up our way of thinking, and adopting His way of thinking. "I have given you an example," He said, "so that you may copy what I have done to you" (John 13:15).

In the Old Testament, perfection consisted in a strict observance of the Law — exterior perfection; but Jesus came and emptied Himself by humility, to give us courage to empty ourselves of our adherence to our own reason and will. This demands an interior change which is more difficult and more purifying than the observance of a law.

Only Faith can give us the conviction and drive to change and give up our own way of thinking and doing — that is, giving our Understanding and Will to God.

"All I want is to know (Understand) Christ," Paul said, "and the power of His Resurrection, and to share His sufferings by reproducing the pattern of His death" (Phil. 3:10).

What is the pattern of Christ's death? When Christ left the bosom of the Father and the Glory of Heaven to become a man, He stripped Himself of all His Glory. He became one of us.

He gave up His way of living as God and took upon Himself a way of living far inferior to His own.

- He had to think as a Man, that man might begin to think as God.
- He had to live as a Man, that man might live as God.
- He had to limit His Power as God, that man might share that Power and become sons of God.
- He had to suffer as a Man, that man might know how he can imitate God.
- He had to show us how to love as a Man, that man might love as God.
- He was content to be limited as Man, that man might reach the limitless.
- He assumed an inferior nature, that man might be raised above his nature.
- He changed, and in changing became Humility itself, that man might realize his nothingness and face the truth with a humble heart.

The pattern of Christ's life was one of denial and sacrifice because of love — love for sinners.

He became Man; He suffered; He died; and He rose, that we might have some definite pattern and way to follow.

We do not have the power to assume another nature, but we do have the ability to change that part of us made to His Image — our soul.

Through Hope and Compassion, we can change depressing emotions to uplifting emotions.

Through Faith and Humility, we can change our way of thinking from a natural level to a supernatural level.

In the Epistle to the Colossians, St. Paul gives us an excellent idea of this pattern of Christian living. It is interesting to see how he alludes to the three keys of Memory, Understanding, and Will.

He says, "You are God's chosen race, His saints; He loves you and you should be clothed in sincere compassion, in kindness (purifying our Memory) and humility, gentleness and patience (increasing our Faith). The Lord has forgiven you; now you must do the same. Bear with one another; forgive each other as soon as a quarrel begins (substituting a good emotion for a bad one). Over all these clothes (Memory and Understanding), to keep them together and complete them, put on Love (the Will purified by love) (Col. 3:12-14).

But what must we do to accomplish this change? St. Paul tells us when he says, "You must kill everything in you that belongs only to earthly life — fornication, impurity, guilty passion, evil desires, and especially greed which is the same thing as worshipping a false god" (Col. 3:5).

We saw as we looked into our Memory and Imagination that all these things came from the heart — the unbridled emotions that defile a man.

St. Paul realized how easy it was to live on an uncontrolled plane. He tells us to destroy these evil emotions and to substitute higher emotions — emotions such as Compassion and Mercy that help change our way of thinking and lead to peace.

He reminded these first Christians that they used to live on a lower level by "getting angry, being bad-tempered, spiteful, using abusive language, and dirty talk" (Col. 3:5).

It is so easy to give in to these weaknesses when everyone else is doing it. We tend to excuse ourselves by considering these attitudes as part of modern-day life — not evil or harmful — only human.

These things are indeed human; they are not divine and we have been called by the Merciful Love of God to rise above these kinds of emotions and replace them with higher ones.

Paul continues, "You have stripped off your old behavior, with your old self, and you have put on a new self, which, will progress toward true knowledge the more it is renewed; in the Image of its Creator" (Col. 3:9-10).

What a magnificent heritage! We have been chosen to think and act like God!

When we begin to substitute God-like qualities for weak, and often evil emotions, we pave the way to clear thinking. Our Understanding arrives at "true knowledge" the more we are renewed.

As we become more Compassionate—enough so as "to forgive as soon as a quarrel begins" (Col. 3:13), and more Merciful—knowing we too have been forgiven, then we will begin "to see what eye has not seen and to hear what ear has not heard" (1 Cor. 2:9).

We saw Peter and the disciples trying to dissuade Our Lord from going to Jerusalem to suffer and die. We realized from this that our dear Lord's physical Presence so blinded their emotions that they became ambitious for high places and desired to live in the favor of the people.

He told them it was *expedient* that He leave them so that the Spirit could come. As long as Jesus was with them, they lived in their Memory and Imagination, and never fully began to live by Faith alone.

They were unable to think the thoughts of God that come through Faith because they were too busy enjoying the Presence of Jesus and receiving the graces that came from that friendship.

It was only when He was gone and they began to live by Faith and in His Spirit that they were able to completely change their pattern of thought and life.

- For a boasting arrogance, they substituted humility.
- For worldly ambition, they substituted a desire for spiritual gifts.
- For impatience at the importunity of the crowds, they substituted compassion for the multitudes.
- For the desire to do everything themselves, they substituted the realization that He did all things in them.

- For the discouragement that followed their imperfections and sins, they substituted peace at the thought of His Mercy.

- For the fear of their fellowman's hatred and persecution, they substituted the joy of following in His footsteps.

Yes, when the Apostles began to live by the example and words of Jesus, they began to change.

- It is true they were filled with the Holy Spirit, but so are we.

- They possessed His Seven Gifts, but so do we.

- They were weak men who were forced by that weakness to strive harder, but so are we.

- They received many graces from God, but so have we.

- The era in which they lived was evil, but so is ours.

- They had the satisfaction of seeing their work signed by miracles, but so can we.

- Their Faith was so great they moved the mountain of paganism, but so can we.

- They saw persecution through the eyes of Faith and suffered with joy, but so can we.

- ✍ They saw things as they really were and not as they appeared to be, but so can we.
- ✍ They had three years of living with Jesus, and His words were written in their hearts, but we have 2,000 years of living in His Spirit, His example clearly written in the Gospels, the witness of His power among men and clear interpretation and lights on His words.

Yes, they had much, but we have more.

We can take courage from the fruit they bore and the example they left us. What a change there was in Peter after Pentecost. When he began to live by Faith, all the potential that was buried beneath his boasting and worldly ambitions began to emerge. It gives us Hope to see men do an "about face" in their way of thinking.

For a few moments let us keep in mind Peter's weaknesses and his effort to dissuade the Master, as we read some of his second Epistle.

He learned not to trust his own strength, and said, "By His Divine Power, He has given us all things that we need for life and true devotion" (2 Pet. 1:3).

Peter learned the hard way that emotional feelings did not always spell out true devotion.

In making these gifts, He has given us the guarantee of something very great and wonderful to come. (2 Pet. 1:4)

This is the same man who witnessed Christ's Transfiguration and was ready to pitch three tents. He had desired earthly consolation to last forever. Now he is content to look forward to a great reward. What it will be he is not sure, but his Faith tells him it is something great, and he is satisfied.

… through them you will be able to share the Divine Nature and to escape corruption in a world sunk in vice. (2 Pet. 1:4)

Now Peter is no longer interested in which one of them is the greatest. He realizes he is called to share the very Nature of God; he remembers his weaknesses and glorifies God's Mercy.

But to attain this, you will have to do your utmost yourselves. (2 Pet. 1:5)

All during the Public Ministry, Peter would ask the Master to increase his Faith, teach him how to pray, explain the parables; and would seek the line of least resistance by asking if he could forgive his neighbor just seven times. Now, he realized God had given him Grace, talents, and Gifts—he had to put forth effort to use them in order to grow in His Love.

> ... adding goodness to the Faith that you have, Understanding to your goodness, self-control to your Understanding, patience to your self-control, true devotion to your patience, kindness towards your fellow men to your devotion, and, to this kindness—Love. (2 Pet. 1:5-7)

Peter had pondered well and realized that one virtue hinged upon another. He found out to his delight that God did want him to contribute towards his salvation, and that when he began to grow in one virtue he would add many other virtues to it. The harder he strove to think and act like God, the more beautiful were the qualities added to his personality. His Memory and Imagination were in control as he substituted other emotions that helped clear his Understanding.

> If you have a generous supply of these, they will not leave you ineffectual or unproductive: they will bring you to a real knowledge of Our Lord Jesus Christ. (2 Pet. 1:8)

Yes, Peter at one time desired but one thing—the restoration of the Kingdom of Israel. He reveled in his power to cure, and rejoiced in the security of the Master's feeding five thousand. Now—he realized that though social problems had to be solved, they were ineffective unless men changed inside.

But without them a man is blind or else short-sighted;
he has forgotten how his past sins were washed away.
(2 Pet. 1:9)

Peter knew from bitter experience just how blind and short-sighted he could be when he lived by the wrong kind of emotions. He lived with the Light for three years, and instead of his humility growing, his self-importance grew, and he forgot his weaknesses and how much of a beneficiary he was of God's Mercy.

Yes, he would remember his past sins, but for regret he would substitute a deep awareness of God's Love and Mercy, and he would grow in humility.

St. Peter realized that if he were to be a man of Faith, if his Understanding were going to see things as Jesus did, he would have to constantly recall His words in order to elevate that Understanding.

"That is why," he said, "I am continually recalling the same truths to you, even though you already know them and hold them firm." This is where many of us fail. Our Memory recalls a truth and our Understanding accepts it, and that is as far as it goes.

We have an idea that a kind of effortless adherence to truth is all that is required of us. Peter may have fallen asleep in the Garden and he may have denied his Lord, but he would never do that again. Now, he would not only listen to God's Word, he would feed his Understanding with that Word.

Peter told the first Christians that it was his duty "to keep stirring them up with reminder" (2 Pet. 1:13). Realizing his departure from this world was imminent, he assured them he would take great care that they would still have a means to "recall these things to memory" (2 Pet. 1:15).

Paul had told his converts the same. He said, "Let the message of Christ, in all its richness, find a home with you" (Col. 3:16). And being a man of deep emotions, he felt that our love and devotion should be expressed with gratitude in our hearts, singing psalms and hymns and inspired songs to God (Col. 3:16-17).

The first Christians gave themselves totally to God. Life was not one long frustration; it was a loving challenge in which they participated in changing their lives from misery to perfect joy.

They strove and succeeded in looking at each situation in life in a new way. They refused to permit themselves to become bogged down in their fears, resentments, anger, and selfish motives.

The Lord had given them Faith and they would use it to rise above the things they could not understand and see them all in His Light.

Human reasoning told the centurion that the Master would have to come and touch his servant and say some prayers in order for him to be healed. But his Faith told him that this Man was God and He had but to Will and it would be done. He chose to live by Faith (Matt. 8:5-13).

Human reasoning told the first Christians that worry was a part of life and they would have to become absorbed in life's problems to solve them. But Faith told them that they were worth more than many sparrows. If they set their hearts first on God's Kingdom and holiness, He would take care of them—so they chose to live in that Faith (Matt. 6:25-34).

Human reasoning told the woman with the hemorrhage that unless the Master looked at her and willed to cure her, she would never be healed. But Faith told her that if she touched the hem of His garment she would be cured. Faith drew power out from Him and she was healed (Mark 5:21-34).

Human reasoning told the first Christians that any change of religion that brought on persecution should be abandoned; that it is important to be accepted by the world. But Faith told them that if they were not accepted in one town they should merely go to another; they were no better than the Master; they should rejoice when they were hated, driven out, and denounced on account of Jesus. It was so with all the holy men of old and their reward was great in Heaven. They chose to live by Faith (Matt. 10:17-25; Luke 5:12).

Human reason would say "if you can't beat the world, join it." But Faith says that we should not fear those who kill the body and after that have nothing else they can do. Faith says we should be happy when we are stripped of worldly goods, for we know we possess something better and everlasting (Heb. 10:32-36).

Human reason would say that you judge a man by his education, his success, his popularity, and his wealth. But Faith says you judge a man by the fruit of virtue in his soul, and though he be poor in the goods of this world, he is rich in God (Matt. 7:15-20).

Human reason says that if someone offends you, you are perfectly justified in hating him. But Faith says that you must "do good to those who hate you, pray for those who treat you badly (Luke 6:27), and forgive seventy times seven.

Human reason says that if we are ill or in pain, it is an evil and a curse from God. But Faith says we should humbly ask to be healed, and seek medical attention to ascertain the method God will choose to heal us. Faith goes even further, however, for it tells us that if after prayer and medical help the illness is still with us, it is an opportunity from God to bring us to patience.

Human reason tells us that we must have displeased God in some way to be visited with so many heartaches and sufferings in our lifetime. But Faith tells us that when we are bearing the fruit of virtue the Father will prune us in order to make us bear more fruit. Suffering is part of our training, for God is treating us as sons (Heb. 12:7).

We can see clearly that as Hope elevates our Memory and calms our emotions it enables us to recall the Words of Jesus and His example. But at this point it is merely a recollection.

It is through Faith that we incorporate that recollection into the present situation, and think, act, and live accordingly.

Unless our Faith has this living quality, what we think is Faith in our life is only Hope — a blind Hope which trusts that God's revelations are true. But Hope alone is not strong enough to change our way of thinking; it only prepares the way. It gives us the courage and assurance that by changing we will arrive at holiness.

This is why the Sacred Writer in the Epistle to the Hebrews says, "Only Faith can guarantee the blessings that we hope for" (Heb. 11:1).

Faith makes the things we hope for real in our lives. They are no longer just words brought forth from our Memory to increase our Knowledge.

They are real, living, and vibrant experiences that change our life from *something* to *Someone*.

And so the Sacred Author continues, "... or prove the existence of the realities that at the present remain unseen" (Heb. 11:1).

Faith truly proves the life and existence of those invisible truths, tucked away in our Memory only as words, and awakened by Hope.

They are raised from knowledge to experience. Sometimes that experience is joyful and sometimes painful, but to the Christian, it is all an experience of Faith.

- Life is always new and fresh because it never ceases to be a challenge in Faith.
- It is never monotonous because it is ever moving.
- It is never satiated because its capacity is unlimited.
- It is never surprised because it penetrates everything.
- It is never in darkness because it always sees the light.
- It is always bearing fruit, in season and out of season, because God is the source.
- It is always secure because its foundation is humility.
- It is never saddened because it drinks of the well of everlasting joy.

Yes, "...a new way has been opened to us, a living opening through the curtain, that is, His Body.... So as we go in, let us be sincere in heart and filled with Faith, our minds sprinkled and free from any traces of a bad conscience" (Heb. 10:20-22).

It is easy to see how one may have a great deal of knowledge of God—knowledge stored in the Memory and released to the Understanding at intervals for speculation and discussion. But that Knowledge may never reach the Faith level.

The World, the Flesh, and the Enemy can all contribute and vie with each other for our attention and adherence.

Jesus speaks of Faith as a power. He said that if we had as much Faith as a mustard seed we could move mountains (Matt. 17:19). Pride, fear, arrogance, doubt, discouragement, and sadness are all mountains that block out our view of God and His Mysteries. Only Faith can remove them. Only Faith in Jesus can say to these mountains, "Remove thyself into the sea" and it would be done (Matt. 21:21).

- Yes, Faith was the power that made the centurion believe in His Word — and the Word healed his servant.

- Faith was the power that made the woman with the hemorrhage believe in His touch and that touch healed her.

- Faith was the power that made the leper believe in His Will — and he heard the words, "Of course I will be made clean" (Mark 1:41-45).

- Faith was the power that drove Peter and Paul and all Christians since, to "struggle wearily on," driven by Christ's own power within them (Col. 1:29).

- Faith is the power that is at its best in weakness (2 Cor. 12:9).

Paul explained it beautifully when he said, "You must live your whole life according to the Christ you have received—Jesus, the Lord; you must be rooted in Him, and built on Him, and held firm by the Faith you have been taught, and full of thanksgiving" (Col. 2:6-8).

So, we are rooted, built, and held firm by our Faith in Jesus. When we recall the parable of the sower we realize the power of Faith. All those who did not bear fruit, had no roots. And if the roots did grow, they withered and were never "built" or "held firm."

Paul gives us a way of protecting ourselves from this danger to our Faith. He says, "Since you have been brought back to true life with Christ, you must look for the things that are in Heaven, where Christ is, sitting at God's right hand" (Col. 3:1).

"Let your thoughts be on heavenly things, not on the things of the earth, because you have died, and now the life you have is hidden with Christ in God" (Col. 3:1-3).

He tells us how to do this in the Epistle to the Philippians. He tells us to be happy, always happy in the Lord—to be tolerant and never to worry.

And then he tells us to pray for whatever we need. Paul is realistic. He knows we are human and need both material and spiritual things, but he knows that our faith in God must be strong enough to realize God's Love and Providence in our regard. We pray and work and He provides.

Paul expected our Faith to be so great that after we have asked we should be full of thanksgiving. Then it is that the peace of God that surpasses all our understanding will be ours (Col. 4:2).

It is that peace, born of a living Faith, that will "guard our hearts and thoughts in Christ Jesus."

"Brothers, fill your minds with everything that is true, everything that is noble, everything that is good and pure, everything that we love and honor, and everything that can be thought virtuous or worthy of praise" (Phil. 4:8).

This is how we are changed into Christ on this earth. Life is full of opportunities to change our way of acting and thinking. Those opportunities can either destroy us or renew us, depending on how we choose to use them.

When we feed our Memory with the Words and example of Jesus, when our Understanding sees His way of thinking and acting, this "sight" is Faith. By spiritual reading, Scripture, and the substitution of unruly emotions with Compassion, we begin to change the material constantly feeding our Understanding.

When that material rises to a higher level, then we begin to "see" people, circumstances, failures, successes, and suffering in a new and different way.

We begin to live, not only as Jesus lived on earth, but as He now lives in Heaven. The difference, of course, is in the Light of Glory and the Beatific Vision.

Both Hope and Faith begin and grow to maturity in this life and are perfected in Heaven.

Hope is perfected by the possession of God, and Faith is perfected by the Vision of God. St. Paul tells us this in his Epistle to the Corinthians. He says, "In short, there are three things that last, Faith, Hope, and Love, and the greatest of these is Love" (1 Cor. 13:13).

It is strange to read that Faith and Hope will last. We ordinarily think that in Heaven they will fall away, and only love remain. But St. Paul fully realized the role of Hope and Faith in our lives. What is begun here on earth is perfected there in Heaven.

What we hoped for on earth in a positive way by raising our emotions to a higher level, we will possess forever. We will no longer have to make an effort to be compassionate — we shall partake of Compassion Itself.

The Memory will no longer have to overcome evil passions, for these passions disappear forever.

The Memory will no longer have guilt complexes to rise above, for we will forever rest in the Mercy of God.

We will no longer feel resentment, only the joy that God brought good out of evil.

Our Hope, given by God, fed by His Gifts, brought forth by trial, and growing through compassion, will have reached its maturity in Heaven by full possession of God. Our Memory will be filled with God forever.

And so it is with Faith. What we saw on earth by changing our way of thinking to a higher and more supernatural way of reasoning, we will see in full light.

Our Understanding, expanding itself by Faith on earth, will see the Mysteries it saw in a dim manner, in the Light of God.

The Understanding that sees reasons for the persecutions of life, through Faith, will experience the reward of those persecutions.

The Understanding that accepted poverty and pain, through Faith, as He did, will know the real value of those sufferings and rejoice in God's Wisdom.

The Understanding that overcame the doubts inherent to its limited nature, by expanding its capacity through Faith in His Word, will be filled with new truths and light for all eternity.

Our Faith, given to us by God, fed by His Gifts, growing through humility, "seeing" His Face everywhere, and experiencing His Power in Life situations, will understand the Mysteries of God. Our Understanding will see God Face to face.

Yes, Hope and Faith abide, but what was only a reflection becomes a reality. St. Paul says, "But when Christ is revealed—and He is your life—you, too, will be revealed in all your glory with Him" (Col. 3:4). Through the Gifts of Faith, Hope, and Love—that is, union with Christ at Baptism—we already live the identical life that He lives in Heaven.

It is not glorious as it will be then, but it is manifested now by the degree of Faith, Hope, and Love we have in this life.

It is so very important that we utilize every precious moment of time. Each moment affords us the opportunity to replace our emotions with His emotions, and our Reasoning with His Reasoning.

Then it is that we shall fulfill the new commandment, for we shall love as He loves (John 13:34).

"So you will be able to lead the kind of life which the Lord expects of you, a life acceptable to Him in all its aspects; showing the results in all the good actions you do, and increasing your knowledge of God.... Now you are able to appear before Him holy, pure, and blameless, as long as you persevere and stand firm on the solid base of the Faith, never letting yourselves drift away from the Hope promised by the Good News" (Col. 1:10, 12, 23).

Our dear Lord Himself gave us the way of accomplishing this, for He said, "if anyone wants to be a follower of Mine, let him renounce himself and take up his cross and follow Me" (Matt. 16:24).

Is the cross that Jesus spoke of only the trials of daily life? No, these form only a part of the cross, for Jesus goes on and speaks of the necessity of changing ourselves and our lives. He says, "For anyone who wants to save his life will lose it; but anyone who loses his life for My sake will find it" (Matt. 16:25).

The type of cross Jesus was speaking of is the interior cross. We might say that renouncing ourselves forms the vertical beam, and the daily vexations of life form the horizontal beam of our cross.

Jesus uses the word "renounce." This means to give up and He is so emphatic about it that we read, in the tenth chapter of Matthew, that unless we do renounce ourselves for Him we are not worthy of Him.

What does He mean when He says that if we want to save our life we will lose it? When we use our faculties for no other purpose than to serve and gratify ourselves, we find only ourselves.

- If a man's Memory never recalls the words and life of Jesus to spur him on to virtue, he is conscious only of himself.

- If a man's Understanding is used only to gratify his pride and selfish interests, he thinks of no one but himself.

- If a man's Will is never united to God's Will, he is totally absorbed in himself.

To spend our lives gratifying our own selfish desires with no renunciation, is to lose God and find only ourselves. The more we give in to every whim, the more we find only ourselves.

We are then conscious of ourselves as every life situation comes along. When we are offended, we are conscious only of how hurt we are, how unjust the offender was, and how best to retaliate.

When we fail, we are conscious only of the feeling of failure, or the part others played in that failure, and we project a hopeless outlook for the future.

When we love, but are not loved in return, we feel bitter, and can become so self-conscious that we never love again.

When we suffer from both spiritual and material poverty, we become so conscious of our privation that we can be resentful and jealous of those who have more material and spiritual gifts.

It is easy to see that when our minds are totally concentrated on ourselves it profits nothing.

In an effort to do everything and be everything without God, we think we are saving ourselves — We want so much to be the master of our fate and the captain of our souls.

In order to arrive at that state that God has destined for us, we must renounce *ourselves* and we must do it for His sake.

Renouncing ourselves must be done for *His* sake, or it again will profit nothing. We have noted how miserable we can be when we are conscious only of ourselves. This misery, however, can drive us to a form of self-denial that is done for no other reason than to replace a bad feeling for a good one.

The motive behind such denial is as selfish and self-oriented as the misery of being absorbed in oneself.

In order to really "find" ourselves, we must be lost in Jesus. Only in Him can we find peace, purpose, joy, and fulfillment. Only when our Memory, Understanding, and Will begin to remember, think, and act like Jesus will we know our true self—the creature God made in His Image.

If we blur His Image by superimposing our own, we will lose our real identity, for we were made for great things, but we insist on clinging to little things.

We so often look at this passage in Scripture about renunciation as meaning giving up food or some other thing in our life.

But Jesus was very emphatic—He spoke of renouncing "self," and myself is all of me—body and soul.

Many people practice great self-denial in food, but their only motive is health. These people would never fast for the sake of the Kingdom.

Body and soul in our human nature are so closely related that one affects the other in everything we do. That is why it is important to control our senses—those windows of our soul—through which our Memory is fed, our Understanding delights, and our Will reacts. So—physical denial is important.

But most important is the denial in our higher faculties, for it is here we are made to His Image, and it is here that we become sons of God. Here is where we must renounce ourselves and put on Jesus.

To renounce in favor of more of the same is not to renounce at all. So, to renounce self for the sake of self is no renunciation.

We do not destroy our faculties by denying them — we renew them, we change them, we rebuild them, and we elevate them to a higher state. But if we insist on keeping our faculties to ourselves under the guise of freedom, then those faculties will sink lower and lower until they are totally distorted and no longer resemble the Image in which they were created.

Only by replacing His way of remembering for our Memory, His way of reasoning for our Understanding, and His Will for our will, can we ever be said to lose our life to find it.

- We "give up" our favorite resentment and put on His Mercy.
- We "give up" our anger and put on His Meekness.
- We "give up" our pride and put on His Humility.
- We "give up" our indifference and put on His Compassion.

- We "give up" our way of looking at things and see them as He sees them.
- We "give up" our own Will and accomplish His Will.

As we do these things day after day, we begin to change. The change is imperceptible and slow but it is constant and sure.

Jesus gave us courage and hope to carry on, though we do not see immediate results, when He said, "This is what the Kingdom of God is like: a man throws seed on the land. Night and day, while he sleeps, when he is awake, the seed is sprouting and growing: how, he does not know. Of its own accord the land produces first the shoot, then the ear, the full grain in the ear. And when the crop is ready, he loses no time: he starts to reap, because the harvest has come" (Mark 4:26-29).

Yes, though we must continue to strive and often do not see or feel results, there is a continuous growth in the image of Jesus in our souls. It is often difficult, but Jesus has told us to shoulder His yoke and learn from Him, for He is gentle and humble in heart; for His yoke is easy and His burden light (Matt. 11:28-30).

Jesus does not want us to carry our burden alone. By assuming our human nature, He has yoked Himself to us, and He wants us to shoulder that yoke with Him.

He has come to dwell in those very faculties that need to be changed, in order to make it easy for us. His grace and gifts are tremendous powers, given to us by His generous Love.

To accomplish this, He had to humble Himself and be meek as a lamb in order to show us the way. Yoked to Him, we change and walk with Him through all the pathways of life. Knowing He did it before us, and that He dwells in our very souls to aid us, we can walk side by side and bear the burden of change together.

If we do not cooperate with God as He bestows many gifts upon us, we shall be like those to whom He addressed these words, "Everyone who listens to these words of Mine and does not act upon them, will be like a stupid man who built his house on sand. Rain came down, floods rose, gales blew and struck that house, and it fell: and what a fall it had!" (Matt. 7:26-27).

OUTLINE 4
To Change as We Share His Nature
We must be Compassionate — MEMORY
To keep our Memory free of Resentment,

To substitute good emotions for bad emotions,
To forgive and forget,
To realize our own weaknesses.
We must be Humble — UNDERSTANDING
To admit our limitations,
To realize His Transcendence,
To accept His Revelations,
To think as He thinks.
We Must be Prayerful — WILL
To have strength to do His Will,
To see things as He sees them,
To prefer Him to ourselves,
To do everything for Him.

Third Key: Will & Love

As our Memory resembles the Father and is elevated by Hope, and our Understanding resembles the Son and is elevated by Faith, so our Will resembles the Holy Spirit and is elevated by Love.

The Love between the Father and the Son is a Person — the Holy Spirit. He is Love and Love is a Power.

Our Will, made to resemble the Holy Spirit, is also a power, and, like Him, it seeks for what is good—it seeks love.

Our Will chooses and puts into action whatever our Memory and Understanding present to it.

If our Memory and Understanding are centered only on ourselves, then our Will ever tends to choose whatever gratifies self.

If we remember only unhappy experiences, and arrive only at unhappy conclusions, then our Will chooses to dislike or hate all those who have contributed to our miserable state. The Will was created by God to choose that which is good, but when our other faculties present only what is bad, our Will begins to choose, and sometimes mistakes what is bad for good.

A man's Will can pursue what is evil, and take pleasure in that evil, if nothing good is ever presented to it. If such a state continues over a long period of time, he can become so hardened in the ways of sin that he chooses evil for all eternity.

God, holiness, and good men can become intolerable to such a man, because his Will has become set on evil.

God has made that Will free to choose between good and evil. Therefore, it is very important that our Will be presented correct information before it makes a choice.

Unless the Will knows Truth, its choices will never satisfy us, and it will vacillate from truth, to half-truth, to no truth at all.

Our free Will is God's most awesome and precious gift to us. It is truly a great power, but like all power it can be used to our advantage, or misused to our harm.

Before we do anything, we must first Will to do it. The action is a result of our Will making a choice. When that Will consistently makes the same choice, it can become habituated in that particular direction.

If a man's Will chooses to drink once or twice, he may still have control over his decision to take another drink. But if his Will habitually chooses to drink, then what was once free becomes enslaved, and the man becomes an alcoholic. Only with great difficulty, and only when his Will chooses to stop, and sobriety becomes a deliberate choice, can he stop what has become an evil habit.

If our Memory and Understanding feed our Will nothing but "self," then we are said to be "self-willed." Everything we do is geared towards gratifying ourselves. We love only those who love us. We tolerate those we do not love, provided they render us a service.

Our one goal in life becomes the pursuit of satisfying all our senses, and our Will begins to choose only those things that promote pleasure, good times, luxury, ambition, and greed. The Will can seek those things to the extent that it chooses them and rejects God.

God, who is Goodness itself, is to such a Will a barrier, for God's Goodness is in opposition to what the Will chooses. A person who possesses that kind of Will runs the risk of rejecting God forever.

What was created in the Image of Love becomes the image of hate. It is still a power, but it is a malicious, distorted power, replacing itself for God.

Our Will, made to resemble the Spirit, Who is Love, must be transformed into that Image; it, too, must be love. To do this, it must draw from its original Source. To be good, it must seek Goodness. To see truth, it must seek the one Truth.

The Memory retains, and the Understanding reasons, but it is the Will that decides what we bring forth from our past, and what course to take when we have come to a conclusion.

It is so important that our Memory be lifted up by Hope, and our Understanding be enlightened by Faith, in order for our Will to always choose the most loving, God-like course of action.

St. John realized this because he said, "You must not love this passing world or anything that is in the world. The love of the Father cannot be in any man who loves the world, because nothing the world has to offer—the sensual body, the lustful eye, pride in possessions—could ever come from the Father, but only from the world" (1 John 2:15-16).

"And the world, with all it craves for, is coming to an end: but anyone who does the Will of God remains forever" (1 John 2:17).

We can look at this passage and think that to love God is a very negative, funless, emotionless adherence to laws and regulations, geared to destroy our free will. But nothing could be further from the truth.

We were created by God to be happy in this life and the next—to possess a "joy no one can take away from us" (John 16:22). But it is our own Will that deprives us of that joy when it seeks those kinds of pleasure for which it was not created.

When a man tries to force a square peg into a round hole, he cannot complain when the corners begin to break off.

God has given us gifts that are pertinent to the faculty upon which they are bestowed. Thus, Hope spurs on our Memory to recall and retain those things that encourage and give us a feeling of assurance.

Faith breaks through the darkness of our finite Understanding and gives us light to see truth as God sees it.

But Supernatural Love is a power designed to elevate our natural love so that our Will can choose a course of action that leads it to greater good.

Here it is necessary to distinguish between natural love, based only on emotions, and supernatural love, based on Faith.

In the previous chapters, we saw our faculties on a natural level: the Memory retaining and recalling, and the Understanding judging, reasoning, and forming opinions.

Our third faculty—the Will—is the power that activates what the other two faculties present to it as being good. The Will, being a strong power and tending towards good, will seek that good at any cost.

The problem is not in the seeking of good, but in the decision as to what constitutes "good."

When man operates only on a natural level, the good he seeks is always purely human. It tends towards self-satisfaction and self-indulgence, since all its faculties are concentrated upon the human person alone.

He may accomplish great exterior works, but those works will never raise him to a supernatural level, for man alone cannot raise himself to a level above his capacities. Knowing this, God has given him Faith, Hope, and Love at Baptism. By himself, man cannot be filled with a participation in God's Nature, which is far above his own nature.

God *is* Love, and unless we grow in *His* kind of love, we shall never bear "the fruit that lasts" (John 15:16).

If we limit our Memory and Understanding to retain and reason only what is natural, then our Will can choose only the things of this world.

This is why God in His Infinite Goodness has given us Commandments and Revelations—to show us what is for our greater good. Our own limited faculties can only choose what is inherent to their own limited capacities, and can never rise to a level far above themselves.

But God, in giving us these elevating gifts at Baptism, leaves our Will free to choose between what we are, which is a limited good, and what He wants us to be—everlastingly Good.

His Word in Scripture does not take away our Will; it merely shows us a more perfect way to arrive at that good which our Will ever desires.

The choice is ours, and when He warns us of eternal punishment, He is not doing so as a hard Taskmaster who demands blind obedience to His Will. No, He merely shows us the end result of a will that seeks its own good outside of God. His Love warns us of the tragic results of the human will seeking its own level.

Since what is finite and limited in its creation, cannot go beyond itself on its own power, it will sink beneath its original level unless God Himself raises it up.

Our faculties, finite at their creation and weakened by Original Sin, must in all humility acknowledge their need and dependence upon their Creator and Lord.

This is the real struggle of life—conforming our Will to God's Will, acknowledging His Will superior to ours, and realizing that, unless He enlightens us, we do not know the way.

There is only one force strong enough to accomplish this, and that is Love, but this Love must be of a higher degree and quality than human love.

This kind of love is greater than the love inherent to our human nature. Human love is limited and finite, and though men have accomplished great things by the ardor of human love, it can never satisfy the human heart. For the human heart longs for a love that is infinite and exclusive—and no human being can fill that desire.

Because our Will resembles the Spirit, Who is Love, it ever seeks greater degrees of love. If it seeks that kind of love in the world or itself, it will always be disappointed and frustrated.

Not knowing where to turn to satiate its desire for love, the Will can seek one finite thing after another, and never find its fulfillment.

Since what it really seeks is beyond its nature and capacity, God has given us Supernatural Love. This love gives our Will free reign to soar into the limitless realms of God's Love and become satiated and absorbed with as much as it desires.

The Spirit, in whose image the Will is made, reveals, through Jesus, the means and the way by which the Will can rise above itself, detach itself, and live in the very Heart of God from whom all good things come.

Thus, Hope raises what ordinarily tends to drag itself down — the Memory. Faith elevates our Reasoning to understand what is beyond its grasp.

But in the Will, which by its nature turns towards good in Love, God has bestowed the same quality except that now the Love that was human becomes a Love that is Divine.

And so the New Commandment is to love one another in the same way Jesus loves us (John 13:34).

And how does Jesus love us? He tells us in the 17th Chapter of St. John. He says, "With Me in them and You in Me, may they be so completely one that the world will realize that it was You who sent Me, and that I have loved them as much as You loved Me" (John 17:21-24).

We are to love with the *love of the Holy Spirit*, for that is how the Father loves the Son, and the Son loves the Father. The Holy Spirit *is* that love. And so it is that God has elevated that faculty—the Will—made only to resemble the Spirit, but now *possessing* the Spirit, Who is Infinite Love.

Now we can love both God and our neighbor with the same love as the Father loves the Son.

Jesus came to make us sons of God, that we may participate in the very love the Father has for the Son. It is infinite, be-yond our wildest dreams, greater than the universe, and deeper than the ocean.

Pride is the rejection of God's love in favor of love for the world and the flesh. Jesus came down to render to the Father a perfect love from a perfect Man. He humbled Himself, taking the form of a slave, to give to the Father what man refused to give—His Will.

In so doing, He showed us the way to eternal life and peace of heart. He is our Model, our Hope, and our Intercessor. We have but to look at Him to move our Will to please the Father.

Without supernatural love moving our Will, our Faith and Hope would come to nothing. Unless we act upon the light that Faith instills, and the assurance that Hope gives us, we will surely be like the man who built his house on sand — because he heard the words of God but did not act upon them (Matt. 7:26).

It is significant that Jesus told His disciples, not all those who say "Lord, Lord" will enter the Kingdom of Heaven, but only the person who does the Father's Will (Matt. 7:21).

To say, "Lord, Lord" is indicative of a degree of Faith, but unless that Faith activates the Will towards God through love, it will be of no profit to the soul.

The Master goes even further and says that even those who have prophesied, cast out demons, and worked miracles in His Name, will not enter the Kingdom, except they do the Father's Will (Matt. 7:21-22).

To acknowledge Him as Lord, and to perform miracles in His Name, presupposes a great deal of Faith. It is frightening to think that one can possess healing charisms and not enter the Kingdom. But we saw an example of this very phenomena in Judas. He healed, as the other disciples did, but he did not do the Father's Will.

His Will was set on personal glory, ambition, and greed, and not on loving His Master and pleasing the Father. Did Jesus try to warn Judas when He said, "Then I shall tell them to their faces: I have never known you: away from Me, you evil men?" (Matt. 7:23).

When we speak of doing the Father's Will, we must understand that what we are really speaking of is Love.

To love Him with a natural love is neither enough nor worthy of Him as God. We must love with a love like His own. He added this new kind of Love to our Will at Baptism, and it is only through giving Him that Will completely that we love Him.

Uniting our Wills to His is more than obedience; it is a union of love — a desire to be like the object of our love — an opportunity to manifest love by preferring Him to ourselves.

Jesus explained this reciprocal love when He said, "As the Father has loved Me, so I have loved you. Remain in My Love. If you keep My commandments, you will remain in My love, just as I have kept My Father's commandments and remain in His Love" (John 15:10).

Jesus is saying that to keep His commandments is to love, and to love is to keep His commandments. He gives Himself as an example of this by saying that this is how He remains in the Father's love. It is by our Will that we keep His commandments, and by that same Will that we love.

One gets the impression that Jesus is telling us a secret, because He says, "I have told you this so that My joy may be in you, and your joy be complete" (John 15:11).

God wants us to be full of joy with nothing missing, and nothing to mar it. He wants to give us His own joy because it is a part of love to see the Beloved joyful—a complete joy that is derived from the source of its love.

If we love God with a purely natural, emotional love, then that love will vacillate in the same way it vacillates in regard to our neighbor. We will love Him when all goes well and we feel His Presence, and be indifferent in times of trial and dryness. Our joy is not complete.

And so it is with our neighbor. When we love our neighbor with only an emotional, natural love, we love when he appeals to our senses, or renders us a service. Our joy is not complete.

To aid us in our quest for complete joy, Jesus repeated His Commandment, and said, "This is My Commandment, love one another as I have loved you" (John 15:12).

Jesus shows His love for us by *remaining* in the Father's love, the source of all love. He said, "The world must be brought to know that I love the Father and that I am doing exactly what the Father told Me" (John 14:31).

In order to love our neighbor then, we must *first* remain in God's Love. And our neighbor will know of that love by the way we keep the Commandments, especially the new one.

This is why, immediately after repeating the commandment to love each other as He loves us, He added, "A man can have no greater love than to lay down his life for his friends. You are My friends if you do what I command you" (John 15:13-14).

The Father asked Jesus to give His life for us, and He obeyed that command. By doing so, He proved His Love for the Father and for us.

We were enemies of God but His obedience to His Father's Will proved His love for us. And that love made us "friends" of God.

We were servants, but Jesus told us that servants do not know the Master's business. The fact that He obeyed the Father's command to live and die for us, makes us friends because He has told us all His secrets.

It is easy to see how closely related our Will and Love are. The kind of Love bestowed upon us at Baptism is the same love the Father has for Jesus and Jesus has for the Father — it is a power capable of making us friends of God, heirs to the Kingdom, and witnesses that Jesus is the Lord.

The first proof then that we love our neighbor is to remain in the Father's love — the source of all love and life. And we do this by keeping His Commandments just as Jesus did.

To accept Jesus as Lord is a commandment, and this is the basis of our Faith as Christians. And this Faith must reach out to our neighbor that he, too, may find God.

That's why Jesus said, "With Me in them and You in Me, may they be so completely one that the world will realize that it was You who sent Me, and that I love them as much as You loved Me" (John 17:23).

The first obligation we have to our neighbor then is spiritual, and the second is social.

That's why the First Commandment is to love God with our whole heart, mind, soul, and strength. To do this, we must *remain* in God's Love. We must keep His words in our heart and choose Him above all things.

The Second Commandment is to love our neighbor as ourselves. This concerns the social aspect or the fruit of our love of God. To love our neighbor as ourselves is to care for him, feed him when he is hungry, clothe him when he is naked, and give our life for him if God so wills.

Jesus Himself showed us very clearly the order in which we should love: God first and neighbor second. And because God is our first love, and the source of our love, our love for our neighbor is *like* our love for God—it is the same love.

He said, "Do you not believe that I am in the Father and the Father is in me?... It is the Father, living in Me, who is doing this work.... Believe it on the evidence of this work, if for no other reason" (John 14:10-11).

What was this evidence? His care for the poor was one of the signs He gave to John the Baptist. His concern for the multitudes when they were hungry, His compassion for sinners, and His healing of the blind and sick, were also signs.

Because He remained in the Father's love, He was able to love His neighbor in the same way He loved the Father; it was with the same love.

Both His Love and His Will were one in the Father, and His Love for mankind was a proof of that love. "Believe in the work I do; then you will know for sure that the Father is in Me and I am in the Father" (John 10:38).

And so it is with us. Our Faith in Jesus must move our Will to love God and neighbor in the same way Jesus does.

Here again, many of us put the cart before the horse. We try to perform good works for the sake of the works. They become our works, and not the works of Jesus in us.

They are not the result of our remaining in His Love like the works of Jesus were. They are often merely acts of kindness that we perform because it is the Christian thing to do.

These kinds of works are only exterior, and their source is ourselves, and though they start out with great zeal, they are, like ourselves, small and without spirit. They do not witness to God's work in us, only to our work in ourselves.

Since the works of Jesus were the result of His remaining in the Father's love, and we are to imitate Him, then our works must be the result of our living in the love of Jesus.

Jesus is our Mediator, our bridge to the Father. As the Son does, so His friends must do. What Jesus is by Nature, He has made us through grace. And this participation in His

Nature—given through Faith, Hope, and Love, and the Seven Gifts of His Spirit—permits us to imitate Him, follow Him, and share in His Sonship.

He became Man to show us the Way. He was perfect Man, and, though He always enjoyed the Hypostatic Union, He experienced all the weaknesses and struggles of our human nature—all except sin.

With this in mind, we must see how God-made-Man used His Human Faculties to show us the Way.

- For Jesus to be our Way, we must look at His Way.
- For Jesus to be our Truth, we must look at His Truth.
- For Jesus to be our Life, we must look at His Life.

There must be a "way" to keep close to God during our daily life, and there is only One who can show it to us—Jesus. We must have a starting point, a map, and direction to arrive at any destination.

Let us say that our starting point is our Memory; our Understanding is our map; and our Will is the direction we take.

The Eternal Word never ceased to be God, as He united Divinity to flesh and blood. He never for a moment forgot Who He was, or the Mission the Father gave Him. But as Man, He did grow in the experience of human weakness, and in this capacity He is able to help us and raise us up above our human level.

To arrive at a proper perspective of the direction our Will must take, we will look at Jesus and see if we can penetrate His secret as to how we can best "remain" in God's Love.

The Way — The Memory of Jesus

St. John says in his Prologue that, "No one has ever seen God; it is only the Son, who is nearest to the Father's heart, who has made Him known" (John 1:18).

We have said our Memory resembles the Father, and we spoke of developing those emotions that are most like the Father—compassion and mercy. We heard Jesus tell us that it is from the heart that the evil desires of man come, and we must be careful because where our treasure is, there will our heart be also.

Jesus is nearest to the Father's heart as God, and He never forgot that position as Man. The Memory of His Father was always with Him and gave Him the courage He needed as Man to withstand the hatred and persecution of His chosen people.

His Memory never left the Presence of the Father. He said to Nicodemus, "We speak only about what we know, and witness only to what we have seen. No one has gone up to Heaven except the One who came down from Heaven, the Son of Man who is in Heaven" (John 3:11-13).

"The Son of Man who is in Heaven" (John 3:13), shows us very clearly where Jesus kept His Human Memory.

Our Memory is a faculty that can keep us in the past, and since our past is of this world, it cannot lift us up above ourselves.

But Jesus kept His yesterday in the Heart of His Father. And He merited Hope for us, so that we may ever keep the Heart of God in our Memory. This can elevate every present moment that so quickly becomes a Memory.

Every life situation must be seen through the eyes of Faith, so that the Memory of that situation may be placed in the Heart of God.

It takes much Hope and Trust to realize that the situation at hand came from God and must be returned to God for care, healing, providing, mercy, and understanding.

It is not for us to worry, to glory in, to regret, or to relive that memory. And when that Memory returns to disturb us or inspire us to pride, we have only to raise it again to the Heart of the Father, Who is Compassionate and Merciful.

Jesus told His enemies one day, "You have never heard His (the Father's) voice or seen His shape, and His Word finds no home in you, because you do not believe in the One He has sent" (John 5:37-38).

It is through the words of Jesus that we hear the Father's words, and we see the Father's shape when we look at Jesus. "To have seen Me is to have seen the Father" (John 14:9).

Those words and that example must be stored in our Memory and recalled often so that the Kingdom of Heaven may dwell within us.

The Memory of Jesus always recalled to His Mind where His teaching came from. "My teaching is not from Myself; it comes from the One who sent Me" (John 7:16). This realization gives us Hope — the One whose words we hear has come from God.

The Memory of Jesus never let Him forget that He was sent by the Father and came from the Father. "I know where I came from and where I am going. . . . I, who am sent by the living Father, Myself draw life from the Father" (John 8:14, 6:57).

The Memory of Jesus constantly fed His beautiful humility. "The One who sent Me is truthful, and what I have learnt from Him I declare to the world.... I do nothing of Myself; what the Father has taught Me, is what I preach.... "What I, for My part, speak of, is what I have seen with my Father" (John 8:26, 28, 38).

Are we saying that to imitate Jesus we must blank life and reality out of our mind? No, Jesus was a realist—the only realist this world has ever known.

He understood human nature, and suffered from every evil that could befall us. He not only saw every situation as it was, but even knew the thoughts of those who hated Him.

He suffered more than any other human being, because He was so perfect and holy, and He understood the evil of sin.

So—when we say that imitating Jesus is unrealistic, we only show our lack of comprehension of His Life and His Mission.

Yes, we must work, live, plan, and provide, but these are not the things that defile us. It is what goes on in our Memory and Understanding and the action of our Will that makes us either realistic or live in a dream world.

A dream is something that may be beautiful or ugly, but whatever it is, it lasts but a moment—and so does life.

Jesus understood this, and kept His Memory of the Father, the Father's Words, the Father's Will, and His Love, Compassion, and Mercy so much in His Mind that it kept Him always in touch with the one and only reality—God.

As Jesus kept the Father in His Memory, we, too, must keep Jesus present in our Memory. He is our bridge to the Father.

Our Memory must recall often that His Words are God's Words. We must remember that when we bear fruit, it is only because we are attached to the true Vine, and it is He who bears fruit in us.

We must recall His burning love for us, as He died for our salvation. We must remember His consoling words in times of need, His warning words in times of temptation, His loving words in times of loneliness, His revealing words in times of doubt, His humble words when tempted to be proud, His reassuring words when tempted to despair, and His pleading words in times of apathy.

As Jesus always saw the Face of the Father, we must ever remember the face of His Son.

As Jesus spoke only the words He heard from the Father, we must speak those words of His Son.

As Jesus taught only what He learned from the Father, we must teach what we learn from His Son.

We must keep our Memory free of all the things of this world — the superfluous things that choke His Words. We must trust and hope in His Words without hesitation, without "ifs" and "buts" and without reserve.

We must keep ourselves free of anger, bitterness, hatred, and self-indulgence, by keeping our Memory occupied with Jesus — His Life — His Presence — His Love.

The Truth — The Understanding of Jesus

The Understanding of Jesus is so far above our own that we catch only a glimpse of it — not because He wants it that way, but because we find it so difficult to think the thoughts of God. We are proud, and that is why humility is so important, in order that our understanding may reason as He reasons, and see as He sees.

Only a humble and childlike heart can understand and accept the words of Jesus.

A proud man lives by his own words, but a humble man — a man of Faith — lives by the Words of Jesus. And because these Words are from Jesus, they are life-giving and enlightening.

"I am the light of the world," He said, "Anyone who follows Me will not be walking in the dark; he will have the light of life" (John 8:12).

From the First Chapter of Matthew, throughout the New Testament, we observe a whole new way of thinking, of understanding, of reasoning.

Jesus was led by the Spirit to be tempted by the devil. The temptations were typical of those we are all plagued with. He had fasted forty days and was tempted to turn stones into bread, but He replied that man does not live by bread alone, but by every word that comes from the mouth of God.

To our human way of thinking, it would have been reasonable to turn stones into bread, especially after a forty-day fast. But Jesus reasoned differently. No — it was not according to the mind of God to use His miraculous powers for Himself.

Most important of all, He used this temptation to raise His Mind to God. God's Word was real food for man's soul, and the "flesh" must never be held in first place. He would give us an example.

Later on in His life, He was to say, "It is the spirit that gives life, the flesh has nothing to offer. The words I have spoken to you are spirit, and they are life" (John 6:63).

At another time, when the disciples returned with food, He said, "I have food to eat that you do not know about.... My food is to do the Will of the One who sent me" (John 4:32, 34).

We see Jesus putting the emphasis on the Spirit. His Memory always beheld the Face of the Father; His Understanding reasoned according to the Words He heard from the Father; His Will was fed by ever being united to the Will of the Father. He fed His Human Soul with the Father's Presence (Memory); the Father's Word (Understanding); and the Father's Will (Will).

The first temptation was directed to His Memory — and emotional faculty. The thought of bread after a fast would arouse His emotions and senses. His hunger was legitimate, but the method suggested to satisfy it was not, and He would not succumb.

The second was a temptation directed to His Understanding. "If You are the Son of God, throw Yourself down; for Scripture says, 'He will put You in His Angels' charge'" (Matt. 4:6). Human reasoning would say, "Yes, You are God's Son, and God has promised to see that You do not dash Your foot against a stone."

But Jesus reasoned differently. He would not take Scripture out of context. His Understanding looked at the whole of Scripture, not at one paragraph. He would see it as God gave it, for it also said, "You must not put the Lord, Your God, to the test" (Luke 4:12). This was a temptation to Pride. The Intellect can be the throne of pride (self), or the throne of God. It can be our home or His Home. We can abide in ourselves, or we can abide in Him.

Jesus would not succumb to the temptation to "show off" and attract the multitudes by some manifestation of His Power—a manifestation that had no purpose but to attract attention to Himself. He would live by the words that the Father gave Him. He came as an Image of the Father's Love and Mercy. He would not swerve from that purpose.

Jesus fed His Understanding with the thoughts of God, and we must do the same. He began His Public Life by immediately giving us new avenues of thought—in the Beatitudes.

The poor in spirit inherit the Kingdom, the gentle inherit the land, and the persecuted are to dance for joy. How contrary to human reasoning!

He said that to refrain from killing someone is not enough; we are not even to be angry or say "Fool" to our neighbor. To refrain from committing adultery is not enough; a man must not even look at a woman with lust. How contrary to human reasoning!

To say we love our neighbors but hate our enemies is not enough. We must also love our enemies—do good to them. How contrary to human reasoning!

He told His disciples that it was necessary that He suffer grievously, die, and rise for our Redemption, and that a loving Father commanded Him to do so. How contrary to human reasoning!

He said if we were meek and humble as He, we would find rest for our souls. How contrary to human reasoning! All of His parables stop our human reasoning short, and we are forced to take another look at God and ourselves. Our way of reasoning concentrates on this life alone, and His way of reasoning sees this life as passing, and looks at everything in its relationship to God and Heaven.

Our human way of reasoning makes us a prisoner in our own house. And this is why Jesus said, "If you make My Word your home, you will indeed be My disciples; you will learn the truth and the truth will make you free. Everyone who commits sin is a slave; now the slave's place in the house is not assured" (John 8:31-35).

Only living in and by His Word are we free, because living by our own words puts us in darkness. So many things in life are riddles, complex, and often tragic. No matter how hard we try, we find no reasons or solutions for them. But Jesus said, "Anyone who follows Me, will not be walking in darkness; he will have the light of life" (John 8:12).

Jesus looked at and reasoned everything in the light of the teaching of the Father. He is the first-born Son and received His information directly from the Father.

We, however, have been given Faith — Faith in Jesus. It is through that living Faith that we receive the teaching and words to live by. It is through Faith — whose foundation is a humble heart — that we begin to Understand and see life in all its facets, with joy and serenity.

"The Father is the source of life," Jesus told His disciples, "and He has made the Son the Source of Life" (John 5:26).

Sometime after He told this to His disciples, He explained to them that unless we received our life from Him we would die. "He who eats My Flesh and drinks My Blood, lives in Me and I live in Him. As I, who am sent by the living Father, Myself draw life from the Father, so, whoever eats Me will draw life from Me" (John 6:56-57).

God became Man — the Incarnation; God becomes food — the Eucharist — Mysteries beyond our poor human reasoning.

As the Son constantly receives life from the Father, being the Son of God, and as He used His human Memory, Understanding, and Will to keep in touch with that life as Man, so we must receive the Eucharist as our source of eternal life, and use our Memory, Understanding, and Will to keep in touch with God through Faith in His Word.

When the Mysteries of God seem too much for our finite minds to grasp, and our Reasoning says, "This is intolerable language. How could anyone accept it?"—let us say with Peter, "Lord, to whom shall we go; You have the Words of Eternal Life" (John 6:68).

Jesus is our source of Life, and we must constantly draw from that Source, or we shall bear no fruit. Jesus told us this when He compared Himself to a Vine and mankind to branches. The Father is the Vinedresser who comes looking for fruit, and when He finds some, He prunes in order to receive a more bountiful harvest.

Jesus was very definite about the source of whatever fruit we manage to bear. "As a branch cannot bear fruit all by itself, but must remain part of the vine, neither can you unless you remain in Me" (John 15:4).

This picture is often brought home to us after a windstorm. The wind or lightning will break a branch off a tree, and in less than a day, the leaves begin to droop, and in another day or two, the branch is dead. It was suddenly cut off from the Source of life.

We can become absorbed in the beauty of branches laden with fruit, and forget the life-giving trunk. And then a windstorm brings us face to face with reality.

And so it is with our spiritual life. Unless we live in Jesus through our Memory, and by Jesus through our Understanding, and with Jesus through our Will, we will wither and die.

Yes, when our Understanding begins to reason as He reasons, we are on our way to being true disciples. Faith is the key that opens our Understanding to higher levels, because Jesus, the Light of the World, is our never-ending source of light.

The Life — The Will of Jesus

From the First Chapter of Matthew to the Prologue of John, we are aware that Jesus is the Lord, and that He came because it was God's Will.

Matthew says, "The Virgin will conceive and give birth to a Son, and they will call Him Emmanuel" (Isa. 7:14; Matt. 1:23). "He will be great and will be called the Son of the Most High" (Luke 1:32).

John says, "who was born not out of human stock, or urge of the flesh, or will of man, but of God Himself" (John 1:13).

God's Will alone brought the Eternal Word into this world, in order for that Word—now Savior—to unite His human Will to the Father's Eternal Will.

Although we are brought into existence by the urge of the flesh, and of human stock,—it is still by that same Will of God that we may unite our wills to His Will.

Though our origin is different, both the Word made Man, and nothingness made man, were born to do the Will of Him who sends them.

Our Will is our most precious possession because it was given as a gift—a gift without strings attached, and a gift that is completely ours to do with as we please.

For that reason it is also a dangerous gift, because we can turn it against ourselves, and in so doing think we are free—free because we do as we please, when we please, and how we please.

St. Peter gave his opinion of all those who think freedom means giving free reign to their desires when he said, "They may promise freedom, but they themselves are slaves — slaves to corruption; because if anyone lets himself be dominated by anything, then he is a slave to it" (2 Pet. 2:19).

This is especially true of Christians who, by their very name, have given themselves to God through obedience to Jesus. It is a contradiction to see a Christian think and act as the world and his own desires dictate.

A Christian who conforms his Will to worldly standards, under the excuse that we live in a modern world, has merely a veneer of Christianity — the truth is not in him.

Of such a man St. Peter says, "Anyone who has escaped the pollution of the world once by coming to know our Lord Jesus Christ, and who allows himself to be entangled by it a second time and mastered, will end up in a worse condition than he began in.... What he has done is exactly as the proverb rightly says: The dog goes back to his own vomit, and when the sow has been washed, it wallows in the mud" (2 Pet: 2:20, 22).

To prevent ourselves from falling into this deplorable state, we will look at Jesus and see how our Exemplar united His Will to the Father's.

Conforming our Will to the Father's Will is the highest exercise of our free will. Jesus Himself showed us this when He said, "I have come here from God; yes, I have come from Him; not that I came because I chose; no, I was sent, and by Him" (John 8:42).

Jesus repeatedly tells us that His aim was not to do His own Will but the Father's Will. "I have come from Heaven," he said, "not to do My own Will but to do the Will of the One who sent Me" (John 6:38).

The Father decided that the Son would be our exemplar and come to earth to live, suffer, and die as any other human being. But to strengthen our faith in Him, He was to rise from the dead.

Jesus was asked to do this—He was sent to accomplish our Redemption—His love for the Father made Him desire only one thing, and that was the accomplishment of the Father's Will.

This is why He could say He was sent, and that He did not come to do His own Will. But because His choice was one of love and union, He could also say, "The Father loves Me because I lay down My life in order to take it up again. No one takes it from Me; I lay it down of My own free will" (John 10:17-18).

It was in His power to lay down His life and take it up again. "This is the command," He said, "I have been given by My Father" (John 10:18).

The more we love, the more we desire to do the will of the Beloved. Love can make us choose the Beloved's Will over and over as a manifestation of our love. It is the best proof of love.

We see this in Jesus throughout the Gospels — so much so that He compares doing the Father's Will to food (John 4:34).

Material food sustains, nourishes, and rebuilds our bodies, and without it our bodily functions would soon be impaired and eventually die. Hunger reminds us of a need for food, and we readily see by loss of weight that we can go just so far without eating.

These are physical signs for physical needs, but the Lord never seemed to be too concerned with this kind of food.

Twice we know He had compassion on the multitudes and fed them in the desert, but when they came after Him, He was disappointed in the motive for their affection.

"You are not looking for Me because you have seen signs, but because you had all the bread you wanted to eat" (John 6:26).

Jesus wants to be loved for Himself alone and not for what He does for us.

This gives us our first clue as to how to unite our wills to God's Will. We must do His Will out of pure love. We are to be grateful for His benefits, but we are to love Him for Himself—because He is God's Son—because He loves us—because He lived, and died for us—because He wants our love —because He is so lovable—and because He is Who He is —our Lord.

"Do not work for food that cannot last," He told them, "but work for food that endures to eternal life, the kind of food the Son of Man is offering you" (John 6:27).

The Words of Jesus are food, and doing the works of God is to believe in those Words. But this is not enough unless, like physical food, these words are taken in and digested.

Jesus added the finishing touch to this process when He said, "My food is to do the Will of the One who sent Me, and to complete His Work" (John 4:34).

To hear and to believe is good, but to complete our work, our Will must act.

Our Will completes the work that our Memory has brought forth and our Understanding accepted.

As it is with the words of God, it is with the words of this world. If our Memory is fed only the words of the world, and our Understanding accepts only the words of the world, then our Will can strive only for worldly gain.

If we live on a constant diet of the words we hear on radio and television, and read in newspapers, books, and magazines, then our Will knows of no other choice to make except what is presented to it. It can choose only the things of this world, and find its good in them. We feed our souls dry straw and slowly starve to death.

How true is the saying that we are what our thoughts are! Just as our bodies become what we eat, our souls become what we hear, see, and do.

We often heard Jesus say that He came to *do* the Will of His Father. To Will is to do, not only to desire.

Whatever we feed our Memory and Understanding makes us *desire*, but the Will must accomplish that desire.

A delicious dinner prepared well, and garnished to excite our appetite, is of no value unless we perform the act of eating. Only then does it become part of us.

We can compare this to our spiritual faculties, for the words we live by must be stored in our Memory, and prepared by our Understanding, but unless our Will acts upon this accumulation of information, it is all useless.

We have an example of this on the night of His Agony. Jesus went into the Garden to pray, and asked Peter, James, and John to pray with Him. He went on ahead to pray alone, but when He came back, they were asleep. He said to Peter, "So you had not the strength to keep awake with Me one hour? You should be awake and praying not to be put to the test. The spirit is willing but the flesh is weak" (Matt. 26:40-41).

Here is our second clue—prayer. Both Jesus and His Apostles were in distress of soul over the prospect of what was to come. The Agony of Jesus was greater because He was aware of every gory detail of the coming Crucifixion.

More than that—He was aware of the stark reality, that even after He showed mankind so much love—love unto death—many would still Will to reject Him.

How were the Apostles to unite their Wills to God's Will at a time when their human nature rebelled against so great a suffering? What do we do when our emotions are at such a pitch that the whole world seems to be crushing in upon us, and our nature cries out in pain and despair?

What do we do when our nature begs for relief and only more distress falls upon it?

When that time comes, we throw ourselves upon the ground of our misery and pray — pray for strength — pray for light — pray for faith — pray that His Will be done, not ours.

This is what Jesus did, and His Will was strengthened; and this is what the Apostles did *not* do, and their Wills were weakened.

Our Will must be strengthened if it is to persevere in its pursuit of the Only Good. Prayer, by its very nature — communing with God — calms our emotions. Our Memory begins to recall the words of God, rather than the words that disturb it. When this happens, our Understanding can see the situation through the eyes of Faith, and our Will, calmed by the prayer, can choose the right course in a more enlightened manner.

Since our body and soul are so closely united, and so dependent upon each other, it seems logical that the process by which the one is fed and strengthened, would also apply to the other.

In order for our body to sustain life, it needs an appetite, food, a preparation of food, a choice of food, and a digestive process. If one of these is missing or out of balance, the body will suffer.

Without an appetite, food becomes intolerable; without food, life is impossible; without the proper choice of food, the bodily functions are impaired; and without a good digestive process, the body suffers great harm.

Our soul must live by a similar process. For appetite, it has desires; for food, Memory; for the preparation of food, Understanding; for a choice of food, the Will; and for a digestive process—prayer.

Rightly did our Lord tell us not to put our hearts in the food that perishes. Material food is fed to a material body and both are destined to perish. But the Words fed to our soul change that soul for good or bad for all Eternity.

And one day when the body is reunited to the soul, that body will take on the beauty or ugliness of the soul. "In the twinkling of an eye... the dead will be raised imperishable ... because our present perishable nature must put on imperishability, and this mortal nature must put on immortality" (1 Cor. 15:52-53).

If we permit the flesh to influence the spirit, the results may not be as evident now, but they will be in Heaven and on the Last Day.

Even though the full impact cannot be seen until the Last Day, we can perceive, from the fruit we bear now, a resemblance of what will be.

We see this in the difference between the fruit Jesus bore and the fruit His Apostles bore.

Let us follow our process and see how it bore fruit and what kind of fruit.

During His life, Jesus had a great desire to Redeem us. He called it a baptism with which He had to be baptized (Mark 10:38).

During His Life, He fed His Memory with the teaching of the Father. His Understanding took that teaching and reasoned out Parables that conveyed word pictures to the people, and revealed the Mysteries of God in the simple words that they could retain.

He saw the Father in every joyous or painful experience, and united His Will to the Father's. He then digested all this Wisdom through hours of prayer and communion with His Father.

When the crucial moment of His Life arrived, His human faculties were able to rise to the occasion and give Him strength.

His desire was ever the same. "Now the hour has come for the Son to be glorified.... Now My soul is troubled. What shall I say: Father, deliver Me from this hour? But it was for this very reason that I have come to this hour" (John 12:23, 27).

His Memory filled Him with sadness and distress. For the first time He pleaded for help. "My Soul is sorrowful to the point of death" (Matt. 26:38). His emotions began to anticipate the suffering to come. Suddenly, He saw all the souls that would refuse His Love. The combination of anticipated pain and rejection brought upon Him a fear that made Him cry out, "My Father, if it is possible, let this cup pass me by. Nevertheless, let it be as You, not I, would have it" (Matt. 26:39).

His Understanding asked if there were any chance of this chalice passing Him by. Even though He had come for this very purpose, was there some remote chance? But, immediately, His Love for the Father prompted Him to say, "Let it be as You, not I, would have it."

He prayed, and He asked the Father the same question three times. Each time, His immediate reaction to His own question was that He preferred the Father's Will.

The important part of this account is the question: How did He sustain His union with the Father's Will, as the answer to His request remained negative?

The answer is: continued prayer. The more His emotions gripped His Soul in fear, the more He reasoned that there might be some slight chance of reversal — and He prayed. And that continued prayer sustained His Will and strengthened it to the point where He could say to His Apostles, "Now the Hour has come when the Son of Man is to be betrayed into the hands of sinners. Get up! Let us go! My betrayer is already close at hand" (Matt. 26:45-46).

Because His faculties had lived in the Father all His life, and prayer nourished His Soul often, He was able in His crisis to remain serene and united to the Father.

The difference between Jesus, His Apostles, and ourselves is evident, and need not be reiterated.

Before He died, He gave us one more secret to help us when life presents us with those unavoidable, unexplainable, and undesirable heartaches — *continued and prolonged prayer*.

Prayer brings our faculties together, unites them in a common purpose, and strengthens our Will to unite itself to God in love.

It is when our faculties are each going in their own direction that the soul becomes confused.

Prayer, a loving thought, and sometimes a rebellious conversation with God, permits each faculty to *take hold of itself* and rest in Him.

This is why the Master often asked His Apostles to go aside and rest awhile. They all needed time to discuss, redirect, and feed their souls with His Words — Words that gave courage, hope, and confidence.

Had the Apostles continued in prayer, as the Master led them to do, they would never have failed Him.

He told them, "You should be awake and praying not to be put to the test" (Matt. 26:41). Is He saying that had they prayed, they would not have to suffer? No, because He prayed, and He had to bear His Cross.

What did He mean then that if they prayed they would not be tested? To be tested is to be given an opportunity to make a choice between two opposites — usually between good and evil, or the right way and the wrong way.

When Jesus told them that prayer would take away the test, He was telling them that prayer would direct their Wills to adhere to God's Will, no matter how difficult or painful it might be.

Through prayer, their spiritual faculties would have remembered the prophecies, seen His Passion through the eyes of Faith, and accepted it with courage. There would have been no test: their Wills, like the Will of the Master, would have been united to the Father; their choice, made in prayer, would have done away with the test.

Not to be put to the test is not the elimination of the cross or temptation: these are part of life. It is being so united to God's Will in every cross that the test is no longer there—it is no longer a choice between good and evil. Our Will, *through prayer*, chooses good and does away with the test, even though the cross remains.

This is why Jesus could get up from prayer, strengthened in His Will, and take up His Cross with serenity. But His Apostles, their faculties dulled by grief, and starved by sleep, were tested and failed.

Having looked at Jesus to see how He used His human faculties, we find that He did everything He asked us to do, and did it under more distressing circumstances than we will ever have.

He never lost sight of the source of His Words—His Father's Face—so His Memory was always at rest. He had trust in His Father's Providence, and never worried when everything seemed to fall apart. He prevented Himself from becoming disturbed by having Compassion on all men.

From the Words He heard from His Father, He Reasoned with the thoughts of God, not men. He saw the value of suffering, detachment, and poverty, and encouraged His followers not to put their trust in the things of this world. His Understanding was always raised to a higher level, and He put the Kingdom of Heaven above everything else. His Humility was unparalleled and as great as His Omnipotence.

His Will, ever fed and guided by a Memory and Understanding filled with the Father, was always united to the Father's Will. His Love for mankind was like the Father's. He loved everyone and excluded no one, no matter how hateful they were to Him. To keep His Will ever united to the Father's, He prayed very much and very often.

We have arrived at a pattern of life that will transform us into Jesus. God has given us human, but spiritual, faculties that resemble His Godhead. He has enhanced them with Infused Virtues to raise them to His level. He has sent His Son to show us how to use them, and He has sent His Spirit to give us Gifts.

Before we go on to find the Master Key, we shall look at our pattern. Let us see how this pattern fits our life:

- Our Memory is elevated by Hope and enhanced by Compassion.
- Our Understanding is elevated by Faith and enhanced by Humility.
- Our Will is elevated by Love and enhanced by Prayer.
- God has given us a Memory and Hope: we must be Compassionate.
- He has given us an Understanding and Faith: we must be humble.
- He has given us a Will and Love: we must pray.
- He has done His part: He waits for us to do ours.

OUTLINE 5
"Turned into the Image That We Reflect" (2 Cor. 3:18)

Memory → A Hopeful and Compassionate Memory → is raised from the image of the Father to being like the Father → "Be Compassionate as your Father is Compassionate" (Luke 6:36).

Understanding → A Humble and Faith-filled Understanding → is raised from a likeness of the Son to Transformation into Jesus → "Learn of Me for I am Meek and Humble of Heart" (Matt. 11:29).

Will → A Loving and Prayerful Will → is raised from a resemblance to the Spirit to Union with the Spirit → "Pray that you be not put to the test" (Luke 22:40).

The Master Key

Our three faculties are like *three keys* that open the door of two different houses. The one is the House of God, and the other the House of the Enemy.

Whichever door they open, in that place they live. That is why Jesus has asked us to make our home in Him, in the same way that He makes His home in us (John 14:23).

The one House is one of beauty, joy, and happiness, and the other is one of ugliness, sadness, and misery. Each one of us has at one time or another lived in both houses alternately. We live in one and then the other, but eventually we find that our stay in one of these houses gets longer and longer.

The Keys were given to us to live only in one House—the House of God, and when we use them to live in the house of the thief, we run the risk of becoming thieves—we take to ourselves what is a gift from a bountiful Father.

We must spend our time using these keys to open many different rooms in the House of God. Though every human being has the *three Keys*, each set opens different rooms, according to the designs of the Householder and the *effort* that the holder of the Keys puts forth.

Yes, in His Father's House there are many rooms, and at this moment He is preparing a place for us (John 14:2-3).

St. Paul was very conscious of the need and effect of effort on our part when he said, "You can build in gold, silver and jewels, or in wood, grass, and straw, but whatever the material, the work of each builder is going to be clearly revealed when the day comes" (1 Cor. 3:12-13).

We can give to God the silver of our Memory, shining with a clear Image of the Father; the gold of our Understanding, bright with the Mysteries of God; and the jewels of our Will, forever united to Eternal Love—or we can develop a Memory of straw, marred by the dead seeds of bitterness; an Understanding like the grass, earthly and low to the ground;

and a Will hard as wood, unyielding and unbending, united to itself in misery.

Whichever set of keys we choose to use, the final product will be seen by the whole world. It is important that we develop these faculties to their highest degree.

We must then determine which one of the *three Keys* is the Master Key, which one opens the door to the others, because without this knowledge we might not use our keys properly.

We have determined that to each faculty God has given a corresponding virtue to elevate it, and a Counsel to develop it.

Faculty	Virtue	Counsel
Memory →	Hope →	Compassion
Understanding →	Faith →	Humility
Will →	Love →	Prayer

In each particular category there is a Master Key — a Key that opens the door to the others in that category — a Key upon which the others depend for development and guidance.

If our pattern is the correct one to follow, then the Master Key in each category should be the area in which that faculty, virtue, and counsel are one.

We will try to prove which combination is the Master Key, and hope the reader will use that Key in his life. Only then will we know for certain that we are using all the Keys and have found the Master Key.

Master Key in the Faculties

MEMORY

We have seen how important it is to keep our Memory free of those memories that feed our soul with disturbing words.

We have seen how Hope elevates, and compassion develops that faculty above itself, to encourage, uplift, and calm the memories that sadden and disturb our souls.

But before we can use any of these gifts and aids, we must *want* to change.

Without the Will to control our Memories, we may cry out in distress and desire to be delivered, but until we want to change, or calm those memories, we will never use the helps God has given us.

"Do not let the sun go down on your anger," the Lord warned us (Eph. 4:26). The words "do not" belong to the power of the Will. It is this power that we use when we "do" or "do not."

We may be ignorant of a way to rid ourselves of bitter memories, but when we seek that way, we are exercising our Will, even though we are not blessed with immediate success.

There are some things we need that we receive for the asking, but there are others that we must seek before we find. An old bad memory may be hard to conquer, but every effort in that direction will fade it out a little more.

If we have spilled ink on a white garment, we may not notice any difference as we begin to blot it out; but continued effort and other helps will make the garment like new — so new, one would never know it was soiled. "Though your sins are as scarlet, they shall be made white as snow" (Isa. 1:18).

As soon as we are conscious of a disturbing memory, we must substitute some words of Jesus, and substitute the feeling of Compassion. A deep realization of our own misery will permit us to have mercy on others. We must also grow in the virtue of Hope, by seeing in a disturbing memory an opportunity to trust God and to gain merit for the next life.

To do all of this, we must *want* to rid ourselves of these frustrating memories. To calm our memories, we need prayer, love, and will power.

Some Memories the Lord Himself will literally take away for the asking. But there are others that are so deep-rooted that His Will permits them to linger—but only for our good.

The exercise of Hope, the practice of Compassion, the prolongation of our prayers, and the effort of our Will towards ridding ourselves of these Memories, all help in changing this faculty and making it stronger.

The continued effort makes our Will stronger to adhere to God's Will in other things; the practice of Compassion makes our whole attitude more understanding and merciful. Through the seemingly fruitless prayer, we actually become more enlightened in the darkness and more "at home" with God.

When the time is over and we have succeeded in conquering that Memory, we will find ourselves more in love with God and more loving to our neighbor.

To conquer bitter Memories with Hope and Compassion then, we need Will Power, Love, and Prayer.

St. Paul tells us, "Never give in then, my dear brothers, never admit defeat; keep on working at the Lord's work always, knowing that in the Lord, you cannot be labouring in vain" (1 Cor. 15:58).

We must *want* to be rid of a Memory; we must *want* to be Compassionate; we must *want* to exercise our Hope. To Want is to Will, and to Will is to do.

We must look at unwanted memories merely as doors, as opportunities to do greater work in that faculty.

St. Paul looked upon every opportunity as a door that opened up new ways of working for God, by changing himself and saving souls.

In the Epistle to the Corinthians, he says, "A big and important door has opened for my work, and there is a great deal of opposition" (1 Cor. 16:9).

St. Paul must have been forced to work on his Memory long and hard, with all the opposition he received. We know from Scripture that when things were hard for him he prayed that his Will would not permit his Memory to conquer.

"Pray for us especially, asking God to show us opportunities for announcing the message and proclaiming the Mystery of Christ, for the sake of which I am in chains; pray that I may proclaim it as clearly as I ought" (Col. 4:3-4).

Paul's memory never let him forget the reason for his persecutions, sufferings, and chains, but he looked upon them all only as opportunities, and prayed that his Will would do as it ought to do — proclaim the word regardless of that suffering.

He appealed to the Memory of these Colossians when he said, "Remember the service that the Lord wants you to do, and try to carry it out. Remember the chains I wear" (Col. 4:17-18). The remembrance of his chains was to give them courage in their own sufferings.

He combines the Memory and Will together to encourage, build, and render a service. He uses this faculty for good, not as a warehouse of evil. Yes, the Memory is our own private, spiritual warehouse, in which our Will can clean house by using the broom of Hope and the dustpan of Compassion.

There are, however, some painful memories that we must retain for our greater good. Peter never forgot his denial because the fruit of that memory was good — it kept him humble, careful, and more loving.

When the time of his own crucifixion came, he used that memory as a tool to encourage him to take this opportunity to show his love for his Master.

Our dear Lord Himself retains His Five Wounds in Heaven. He showed them to His Apostles to prove He had risen. We shall find new joy in Heaven each time we gaze upon them.

They will be glorious reminders of the great Love God has for us.

Our Memory will abide with us in Heaven, but it will be changed. The Memory of our sins will make us glory in His Mercy, and we will rejoice in the power that was so manifest in weakness.

In Heaven we will use our Memory in the way God intended us to use it. We will see the reasons for our trials and how great the reward for so little effort on our part. We will be full of love, joy, compassion, and praise for all Eternity.

God desires that we begin on earth what we shall do in Heaven. Our Memory must see the reasons for our difficulties through the eyes of Faith, and be filled with the same compassion and love as we shall have in Heaven. No hatred, bitterness, resentment, or jealousy must be permitted a place in the warehouse of our Memory.

Because we are in the state of pilgrimage, and our Will is in the state of merit, it will always take effort on our part to keep our Memory in order. But it will be easier as we form the habit of living by our Will, and not by our Memory.

The Sacred Writer says in the Epistle to the Hebrews, "God would not be so unjust as to forget all you have done, the love you have for His Name, or the services you have done, and are still doing for the saints. Our one desire is that every one of you should go on showing the same earnestness to the end" (Heb. 6:10-11).

Here we see God's Memory never forgetting how much effort we put forth for the Kingdom, and how we should use that Eternal Memory as a tool to prod our Will on to greater work for the Kingdom. He forgets our sins but always remembers the good we do.

Paul said to Titus, "Remember, there was a time when we were ignorant, disobedient, and misled, and enslaved by different passions and luxuries; we lived then in wickedness and ill will, hating each other and hateful ourselves" (Titus 3:3).

What a perfect example of someone living in an uncontrolled Memory. But why did he ask that we remember those weaknesses? "It was not because He was concerned with any righteous actions we might have done ourselves; it was for no reason except His own compassion that He saved us by means of the cleansing water of rebirth (Baptism) and by renewing us in the Holy Spirit..." (Titus 3:5-6).

God Himself remembers our good works, our desires, and our effort, and His Mercy in our regard is guided by His Compassion, not by our goodness. And so it must be with us on earth.

Our Compassion for our neighbor must ever keep before our eyes his effort and desires and not dwell upon his weaknesses. We must love our neighbor because we want to be good, not because he is good. That is how God loves us. We must then keep before the eyes of our Memory our neighbor's good deeds and not his sins and weaknesses.

To do this, we need Will power, love, and prayer, for this is how God treats us in regard to His Memory. He has Compassion on our weakness because He wants to, because He loves us, because He thinks of us constantly.

This is to be perfect as He is perfect.

- He no longer remembers our sins—we should not remember the sins of our neighbor.
- He remembers our effort, good deeds and services—we should remember the good our neighbor accomplishes.
- He does this because He is good, and not because we are good—we should do this, too, because we want to be good, not because our neighbor is good.
- He Wills to love us even when we are sinners—we should Will to love all men even when they offend us.
- His Eternal thought of us keeps us in existence; our conversation with Him keeps our soul united to Him.

As we do to our neighbor in regard to our Memory, we must do to ourselves. We must be compassionate with ourselves, acknowledging our efforts even though we possess many weaknesses.

We must remember the good in the past, and have compassion on our limited abilities until we grow in virtue.

We must love ourselves, not because we are always lovable, but because He lives in us and we are His sons. We must have courage and understand that we can do all things in Him who strengthens us.

Yes, we must use our Memory in regard to ourselves and our neighbor in the same way God uses His Memory in our regard, with Compassion and Love through union of our Wills with His. This demands virtue.

Jesus said that on the last day He will remind us that when He was sick we visited Him (Matt. 25:36). It is significant to note that He said "visited" and not "healed" Him.

There are some illnesses and some memories that God may not take away because they have healing powers in themselves.

We learned this truth in Peter's life after Pentecost. The thought of his denial healed his boasting and pride. It helped change an ambitious man into a man of understanding and compassion. And so it is with us. We can be assured that if we have a distressing illness or Memory the Lord has not taken away, it has spiritual healing powers hidden within, and only Faith will unlock those doors.

It takes more Compassion and Faith to see and profit from a long illness or Memory than it does to be cured of that distress. Here again, our Will must be united to God's Will and know that if we believe we shall be healed. But our healing will be in the area that is the most profitable for our eternal glory.

This brings us to our Understanding level, and we shall see if the "Will" opens this door as it did the door of the Memory.

UNDERSTANDING

Our ability to reason is a most precious gift and yet it is limited—limited in its ability and capacity. But God again, by adding Faith, has given it the ability to go beyond itself to limitless regions of intellectual light.

Faith in Jesus, given to us at Baptism, makes us sons of God, as we see beyond the visible creation into the invisible creation. This new ability is enhanced greatly by humility the virtue that makes us "decrease so He may increase" (John 3:30).

But here, too, we must "want" to see Jesus and be Jesus if our Faith is to go beyond the belief stage.

St. Paul told the Romans, "Faith leads to faith, or, as Scripture says: The upright man finds life through Faith" (Rom. 1:17). Faith must grow out of the seed of belief, to a great tree, whose roots are humility and whose fruits are good works.

"Christians are told by the Spirit," Paul says, "to look to Faith for those rewards that righteousness hopes for... what matters is Faith that makes its power felt through love" (Gal. 5:5-6).

Our Will is a "power" whose elevating Virtue is Love, and that power is felt by our soul as it is elevated into the regions of God through Faith.

That power makes our Faith branch out into good works, and raises our Understanding to heights beyond its human capacity.

The human Will must unite itself to the Divine Will in all His revelations—revelations that stagger the human Understanding. The Will must reach out and accept the truths presented to it through Faith, wrap them in deep Love, and express them to our neighbor by good works.

Since God's Nature is so far above our own, and it is only through Faith that we can live in Him, then it is through prayer that we become more accustomed to the pure air of Faith—so pure is that air that we can breathe in only small amounts at a time until we begin to change and are able to breathe freely as we see God Face to face in Faith.

Jesus warned His Apostles that if they did not pray they would be put to the test. "You will all lose faith in Me this night" (Matt. 26:31). Christ's Crucifixion would prove an obstacle to their Faith because they refused to unite their Wills to God's Will as to "how" God would redeem mankind.

They wanted Him to redeem us in a blaze of glory, and not through the ignominy of the Cross—the Cross—an obstacle to the Jews and madness to pagans (1 Cor. 1:23).

For Faith to grow, we must want to believe, not because we fully comprehend, but because the Mysteries we accept come from God. Faith, united to our Will, is a power that can move a mountain. Our Will, united to Faith, and Love, can move the Heart of God.

The more we want to do God's Will, and accepting Jesus is His Will, the more Faith we will possess and the deeper will be our love. Without the power of our Will behind our Faith, love would never flourish.

Paul realized this when he said, "If I have Faith in all its fullness, to move mountains, but without love, then I am nothing at all" (1 Cor. 13:2).

Our Faith must rise above the knowledge level of believing in Jesus, to the Will level of loving Jesus, or it is fruitless.

This is why St. James said, "You believe in the one God; that is credible enough, but the demons have the same belief, and they tremble with fear" (James 2:19).

It is not enough to believe that Jesus is Lord. We must "want" to love Him more than ourselves. We must unite our Will to His Will; we must love Him with our whole heart, mind, soul, and strength; and we must converse with Him often and long—to praise, adore, thank, and ask.

As Faith opens the door of our Understanding, and Humility increases that Faith, the Will—with its Love and Prayer—opens these doors wider and wider until all of Heaven lives in us. Yes, the Will opens the door of our Understanding to make our Faith fruitful in good works, and capable of changing our way of reasoning to His way of reasoning. It teaches us to think the thoughts of God.

WILL

We have seen how the Will and its accompanying virtues open the door to both Memory and Understanding, but we have yet to establish what the Will does for itself.

God gave us all ten talents when He created us to His Image. He added eighty more talents when He bestowed upon us Faith, Hope, and Love. But we must gain those other ten talents if we are to be perfect.

No matter how much a father does for a child, unless that child shows some initiative in regard to his gifts, those gifts will lie dormant.

This is why the Will is so important and why Jesus spoke so much about doing God's Will, keeping His Word, and making our home in Him. To do, to keep, to make, to abide, and to unite, are all words that show the necessity of doing our part in gaining the Kingdom. We must *want* God; we must *choose* God: and we must *love* God if we are to live with Him forever.

These are all the things the faculty of the Will can accomplish for us. What a power the Will is! How much we desire to hold it for our very own! How much we desire to have God do our Will! How much we desire others to do our Will!

We hold on to it with a tenacity that defies description, and we will fight and die to keep it free.

- The Will made martyrs endure torture rather than deny their Lord.
- The Will makes us push forward, seeking God, though our weaknesses make us feel it is impossible to reach Him.
- The Will enables us to overcome evil habits and replace them with good ones.
- The Will makes us seek the Kingdom no matter what the cost.
- The Will enables us to love, even when those on whom we bestow this gift are ungrateful and unlovable.
- The Will is a power that enables us to unite a finite Will with a Divine Will, and in so doing be transformed into Jesus.

But when we keep this power to ourselves and never seek to unite it to Infinite Power in Love, it is confined in the small area of the soul, and eventually explodes, throwing the soul in any and every direction. It seeks pleasure, sin, pride, hate, and anything else that keeps it in a whirlwind of unharnessed power.

It carries us into places we do not want to go, and makes us do things we do not want to do. We are tossed to and fro like a buoy on the sea, always moving yet ever staying in the same place.

St. Paul told the Romans: "I cannot understand my own behavior. I fail to carry out the things I want to do, and I find myself doing the very things I hate.... What a wretched man I am!" (Rom. 7:15, 24). Paul had to struggle, as we all struggle, with two opposing forces locked inside of us—one desiring an Infinite Good that is spiritual, and the other, a finite good that is material.

Paul finally came to grips with this paradox and said, "The unspiritual are interested only in what is unspiritual, but the spiritual are interested in spiritual things" (Rom. 8:5).

"People who are interested only in unspiritual things can never be pleasing to God. Your interests, however, are not in the unspiritual, but in the spiritual, since the Spirit of God has made His home in you" (Rom. 8:5, 8-9).

Our Will, made to resemble the Holy Spirit, will never find rest until it is at home in Him. The Holy Spirit is Love, and our Will, elevated by His Love at Baptism, must be united to Him by being one with Him.

"The Spirit Himself and our spirit bear united witness that we are children of God" (Rom. 8:16).

Our Will must be sensitive to His Will in our lives, and Paul tells us how to discern that Will by recommending Love and Prayer. He says we must remember that in all the trials of life, God turns everything into good for those who love Him (Rom. 8:28).

Our Will vacillates and rebels because it does not see the good in our sufferings. It seeks its own way, determined that it is better than God's way.

Our Will must be one with God, and when we feel too weak to carry on, Paul tells us, "The Spirit comes to help us in our weakness. For when we cannot choose words in order to pray properly, the Spirit Himself expresses our plea in a way that could never be put into words" (Rom. 8:26).

The Spirit strengthens our Will at a time when it is weary with its struggle to be one with Him. Paul constantly implored his converts to pray, to pray for strength, to pray in time of illness, to pray for the faithful, to pray for spiritual gifts, to pray in times of trial, to pray for humility and generosity, and, most of all, to thank God for His benefits.

It is the love that comes through prayer that enables the Will to keep itself united to God at all times and in all circumstances.

Prayer keeps the flame of love burning bright in our hearts; it keeps us aware of the Presence of the Divine Spirit living within us; it permits us to speak to God as a son to a father; and it keeps His Words ever before us to encourage our Will to follow the Spirit.

Prayer assures us that "nothing can come between us and the love of Christ, even if we are troubled or worried, or being persecuted, or lacking food or clothes, or being threatened, or even attacked" (Rom. 8:35).

Paul's Will was so united to God's Will—even though he had to struggle at times to keep it so—that he said, "For I am certain of this: neither death nor life, no angel, no prince, nothing that exists, nothing still to come, not any power, or height or depth, nor any created thing, can ever come between us and the love of God made visible in Christ Jesus, our Lord" (Rom. 8:38-39).

He had learned to mistrust his own Will, so prone to deceive him, and to trust in God's designs for him as expressed by every day occurrences.

He learned the hard way "how rich were the depths of God, how deep His wisdom and knowledge, and how impossible to penetrate His motives or understand His methods" (Rom. 11:33).

He would be humble and acknowledge his inability to comprehend God's work in his soul, but he would change as the Divine Sculptor desired.

"Do not model yourselves on the behavior of the world around you, but let your behavior change, modeled by your new mind. This is the only way to discover the Will of God and know what is good, what it is that God wants, what is the perfect thing to do" (Rom. 12:2).

A "new mind" is the mark of a real Christian. He thinks and acts like God, and when he fails, he glorifies God by an unbounded hope in His Mercy. His Will, ever tending towards God, takes advantage of every moment of life to increase its thrust into God.

The Will, elevated by the Spirit of Love, and strengthened by a filial relationship with God in prayer, opens the doors of our faculties to new horizons.

It is the Master Key that changes our Memories by a spirit of Hope and Compassion, raises our Understanding to the realms of Faith through Humility, and unites itself to the power of the Spirit through Love and Prayer.

- ☙ The Will opens every door and its own door because it is a power that nothing in the soul can resist.
- ☙ Memory, Understanding, and Will, these three, but the greatest of these is Will.
- ☙ Faith, Hope, and Love, these three, but the greatest of these is Love.
- ☙ Compassion, Humility, and Prayer, these three, but the greatest of these is Prayer.

Will, Love, and Prayer, these three — the Master Key.

PRAYER

Compassionate Father, I put all my Hope in Thee. Purify my Memory and root out everything that keeps me from Thee. Let the remembrance of Thy Merciful Love in my regard make me compassionate to my neighbor so that like Thee I may extend my love to all men.

Humble Jesus, I put all my Faith in Thee. Purify my Understanding, and let me rise above my limited intellect and accept the wonders of Your Revelations with a humble heart.

Three Keys to the Kingdom

Loving Spirit, I put all my Love in Thee. Purify my Will that it may be united to the Father's Will in all things, and my being transformed into Jesus by the peace of Thy Love.

The author prays that all those who read this booklet will have a deeper awareness of the Father's Mercy, the Son's Love and the Spirit's Power.

MOTHER M. ANGELICA

(1923-2016)

Mother Mary Angelica of the Annunciation was born Rita Antoinette Rizzo on April 20, 1923, in Canton, Ohio. After a difficult childhood, a healing of her recurring stomach ailment led the young Rita on a process of discernment that ended in the Poor Clares of Perpetual Adoration in Cleveland.

Thirteen years later, in 1956, Sister Angelica promised the Lord as she awaited spinal surgery that, if He would permit her to walk again, she would build Him a monastery in the South. In Irondale, Alabama, Mother Angelica's vision took form. Her distinctive approach to teaching the Faith led to parish talks, then pamphlets and books, then radio and television opportunities.

By 1980 the Sisters had converted a garage at the monastery into a rudimentary television studio. EWTN was born.

Mother Angelica has been a constant presence on television in the United States and around the world for more than thirty-five years. Innumerable conversions to the Catholic Faith have been attributed to her unique gift for presenting the gospel: joyful but resolute, calming but bracing.

Mother Angelica spent the last years of her life cloistered in the second monastery she founded: Our Lady of the Angels in Hanceville, Alabama, where she and her Nuns dedicated themselves to prayer and adoration of Our Lord in the Most Blessed Sacrament.